Michelle Nietert, MA, LPC-S, AND Lynn Cowell

Strong and Secure

ZONDERVAN

ZONDERVAN

Strong and Secure
Copyright © 2025 by Michelle Nietert and Lynn Cowell

Published in Grand Rapids, Michigan, by Zondervan. Zondervan is a registered trademark of The Zondervan Corporation, L.L.C., a wholly owned subsidiary of HarperCollins Christian Publishing, Inc.

Requests for information should be addressed to customercare@harpercollins.com.

Zondervan titles may be purchased in bulk for educational, business, fundraising, or sales promotional use. For information, please email SpecialMarkets@Zondervan.com.

ISBN 978-0-310-14407-6 (hardcover)
ISBN 978-0-310-14422-9 (audio)
ISBN 978-0-310-14421-2 (ebook)

Library of Congress Cataloging-in-Publication Data
LC record available at https://lccn.loc.gov/2024016849
LC ebook record available at https://lccn.loc.gov/2024016850

Unless otherwise indicated, Scripture quotations are taken from The Holy Bible, New International Version®, NIV®. Copyright © 1973, 1978, 1984, 2011 by Biblica, Inc.® Used by permission of Zondervan. All rights reserved worldwide. www.Zondervan.com. The "NIV" and "New International Version" are trademarks registered in the United States Patent and Trademark Office by Biblica, Inc.®. Scripture quotations marked AMP are taken from the Amplified® Bible (AMP). Copyright © 2015 by The Lockman Foundation. Used by permission. www.lockman.org. Scripture quotations marked CEV are taken from the Contemporary English Version. Copyright © 1991, 1992, 1995 by American Bible Society. Used by permission. Scripture quotations marked CSB are taken from the Christian Standard Bible®. Copyright © 2017 by Holman Bible Publishers. Used by permission. Christian Standard Bible® and CSB®, are federally registered trademarks of Holman Bible Publishers. Scripture quotations marked ESV are taken from the ESV® Bible (The Holy Bible, English Standard Version®). Copyright © 2001 by Crossway, a publishing ministry of Good News Publishers. Used by permission. All rights reserved. Scripture quotations marked GNT are taken from the Good News Translation in Today's English Version—Second Edition. Copyright 1992 American Bible Society. Used by permission. Scripture quotations marked MSG are taken from *THE MESSAGE*. Copyright © 1993, 2002, 2018 by Eugene H. Peterson. Used by permission of NavPress. All rights reserved. Represented by Tyndale House Publishers, Inc. Scripture quotations marked NASB are taken from the New American Standard Bible® (NASB). Copyright © 1960, 1962, 1963, 1968, 1971, 1972, 1973, 1975, 1977, 1995 by The Lockman Foundation. Used by permission. www.lockman.org. Scripture quotations marked NCV are taken from the New Century Version®. Copyright © 2005 by Thomas Nelson. Used by permission. All rights reserved. Scripture quotations marked NLT are taken from the Holy Bible, New Living Translation. © 1996, 2004, 2015 by Tyndale House Foundation. Used by permission of Tyndale House Publishers, Inc., Carol Stream, Illinois 60188. All rights reserved.

The information in this book has been carefully researched by the author, and is intended to be a source of information only. While the methods contained herein work, readers are urged to consult with their physicians or other medical and mental health professionals to address issues. The author and the publisher assume no responsibility for any injuries suffered or damages or losses incurred during or as a result of the use or application of the information contained herein.

Any internet addresses (websites, blogs, etc.) and telephone numbers in this book are offered as a resource. They are not intended in any way to be or imply an endorsement by Zondervan, nor does Zondervan vouch for the content of these sites and numbers for the life of this book.

All rights reserved. No part of this publication may be reproduced, stored in a retrieval system, or transmitted in any form or by any means—electronic, mechanical, photocopy, recording, or any other—except for brief quotations in printed reviews, without the prior permission of the publisher.

Lynn Cowell and Michelle Nietert are represented by the literary agency of The Blythe Daniel Agency Inc., Post Office Box 64197, Colorado Springs, CO 80962.

Cover design: Micah Kandros/Micah Kandros Design
Interior design: Denise Froehlich

Printed in Malaysia

25 26 27 28 29 30 31 / OFF / 10 9 8 7 6 5 4 3 2 1

To Cassie, Jo, Katy, Laurli, Megan, and Rachel: Thank you for being the first girls to dig into God's Word with me. LIGHT, with you all, was such a joy for me!

LOVE, LYNN

In loving memory of my father, Mike Holman, known to many as "Missionary Mike," for introducing me to our heavenly Father during my childhood, and in honor of Reggie McNeal, who modeled for me the love and assurance of Father God during my high school, college, and church staff years.

MICHELLE

Contents

Introduction to Your Father

The rustic coffee table had been in our family's TV room for many, many years, but now it was time for it to go to a new owner. I dumped out each drawer's contents. That's when I saw a little book that said *To Grandma, with Love* on the cover. It had been written by my cousin decades ago, and before I knew it, I had spent an entire afternoon reading about a grandma I had never truly known. Through interviews with Grandma, as well as those who lived life with her, my cousin described the tragedies and highlights of Grandma's life. Grandma had clearly adored my cousin, and my cousin adored her in return. To my surprise, I discovered that the more I learned about my father's mother, the more I learned about myself. I even learned a little about why I do the things I do, because I am her granddaughter.

In a way, this is what Michelle and I hope will happen as you read *Strong and Secure*. In this devotional about knowing God as our Father, you can learn more about God, how He describes Himself, what other people say about Him, as well as how He interacts with people. As you learn more about who God is, you'll learn about yourself and who you are as His daughter.

How? you wonder. The more we know our Father, the stronger we will be in life. You can become secure in your faith, let go of your doubts, and receive reassurance that He loves you, is there for you, and is working in your life. When we *know* our heavenly Father, our anxiety calms. Racing minds slow down. Rest comes. Experiencing the Father as our

Protector, Healer, Peace-giver, and Provider allows us to become familiar with His presence and feel like we're finally "home."

I have a sweet memory of my youngest daughter when she was a teenager. She came downstairs in the early hours of the morning to find me in my office. There, she curled up on the floor by my chair, pillow under her head, blanket wrapped around her body. Comfortable once again, she drifted back to sleep.

This is what Father God has for us: Comfort in His presence. Freedom from anxiety. Safety in belonging to Him. This kind of relationship is even made clear in the name Jesus used for God in Mark 14:36—calling Him **Abba,** a word that signaled Jesus's absolute trust, closeness, and connection with His Father.

As you read *Strong and Secure*, keep in mind that knowing God as Abba takes time.

Think about when you first met your best friend. Did you feel the same way on that day as you feel about them today? Probably not. Getting to know someone takes time. The same is true with God: as we take time to learn more about our Father, we will know Him more deeply than we do today.

I also encourage you to think about how you act around the people you know and love dearly. Do you try to spend as much time as you can with them? Do you like just being near, like my daughter in my office? Or with people you're very close to and trust, do you even hold hands or touch their arm to let them know you care?

Our Abba Father wants us close to Him—as close as we can get. Snuggled up close. Don't be afraid. He won't become distracted by something else or leave you. He is here to spend time with you.

And while we have no idea what each day will hold, we can rest assured that whatever it is, our heavenly Father is with us, ready to love and support us no matter what.

How to Use
Strong and Secure

Step 1: Read

Each day, you'll find a new devotion with a Bible verse at the very beginning. Always start with reading God's Word—the most important words. Next, read the devotion, taking your time. Let your Father speak to you through the words on each page. If something interesting stands out to you, grab a pen or highlighter and mark it so you remember.

Step 2: Reflect

When you've finished the devotion for the day, you'll see a section called "Experiencing Father God's [Protection/Healing/Peace/Provision/Presence]." This section will help you apply what you read to your life. It might ask you a question or offer a thought to think on for the day or even provide a space to journal. If you can't answer the question right away, that's okay. Come back to it when you're ready.

Some days there is a prayer to pray. When we pray, we can begin with **Father** just like Jesus did. In fact, when He taught His disciples to pray, Jesus started His prayer with "Our Father." Doing the same will help reinforce to our hearts that He is our good Father (Mark 14:36, Romans 8:15, Galatians 4:6).

Step 3: Growing Stronger

After you've completed the "Experiencing Father God" section, you'll find a section called "Growing Stronger." This is for learning more, developing a deeper relationship with Father God, and growing stronger. It may include additional Scripture passages to help you dig into God's Word on your own or offer a challenge to help you understand and move closer to your Father's heart.

Step 4: Memorize Scripture

At the beginning of each section, you'll see a page called "Meditation Matters." **Meditation** is simply thinking about something without being distracted. So when we meditate—or think about—Scripture, it's a really cool way for us to connect with God! You can refer back to these pages at the end of each day as a way to read, meditate, and memorize Scripture.

My favorite way to memorize God's Word is to type the verse into the Notes app in my phone. I read these verses while I get ready in the morning, eat breakfast, wait in my car, or anytime I might usually look at social media. It is a great way to fill my heart with the Father's love! At the counseling center, we encourage clients to use a sticky note to write down the verse they are memorizing to help them overcome a struggle. Usually, they make many of these to place on a mirror where they dry their hair, by the sink where dishes are washed, and even on a steering wheel where they can rehearse the verse at stoplights.

Protector

MEDITATION MATTERS

For in the day of trouble he will keep me safe in his dwelling; he will hide me in the shelter of his sacred tent and set me high upon a rock.

PSALM 27:5

But you, God, see the trouble of the afflicted; you consider their grief and take it in hand. The victims commit themselves to you; you are the helper of the fatherless.

PSALM 10:14

Trust God, my friends, and always tell him each of your concerns. God is our place of safety.

PSALM 62:8 CEV

The LORD is compassionate and gracious, slow to anger, abounding in love.

PSALM 103:8

1

Abba Father

MICHELLE

The Spirit you received does not make you slaves,
so that you live in fear again; rather, the Spirit
you received brought about your adoption to
sonship. And by him we cry, "Abba, Father."

ROMANS 8:15

*A*s little girls, we learn that being good gets us smiles—from our parents, our friends, our teachers. We hear words of praise, and we love the positive attention our good deeds bring us. Many of us learn from these experiences that the key to being happy is to be really, really good at everything we do. As we mature and life demands more of us, the pressure intensifies. This pressure often creates responses like, "I hate feeling like I have to be perfect; if I make one mistake, my entire life will be ruined."

The drive to be perfect can create a level of fear that leads to anxiety. And that anxiety leads us to feel one of two ways: hypervigilant, where we make sure nothing goes wrong, or helpless, where trying doesn't seem to matter. Both can lead us to procrastinate or feel like giving up.

Father God wants to protect us from the oppression that the need to be perfect brings. He does this by allowing us to be part of His family and His rules. His rules aren't about us being good; instead, He focuses on us being loved. When we become part of God's family by trusting in Jesus, we get to call the God of the universe "Father." Your Father God wants you to know His unconditional love for you—no matter what you've done or how badly you believe you've messed up.

Experiencing Father God's Protection

The next time you feel like you are going to mess up—or you already have—turn to God as a loving Father who isn't disappointed in you but instead loves you and wants to be close to you. Imagine your heavenly Father there with open arms even when you sin against Him, you get a bad grade on a test, you hang out with the wrong crowd, you make the wrong choice, or you ignore Him for a long time. He's still there for you, and you are still His girl. God forgives you not because of anything you've done but because of who you are and who He is—your Father. His family is forever.

Growing Stronger

In your Bible, read Mark 14:36 and Galatians 4:6. These verses show two other times the word **Abba** is used in Scripture.

2

You've Seen Me; You've Seen the Father

LYNN

Jesus answered: "Don't you know me, Philip, even after I have been among you such a long time? Anyone who has seen me has seen the Father. How can you say, 'Show us the Father'?"

JOHN 14:9

I love when the Bible records people and their struggles with doubting, their lack of understanding, and their questions. It makes me feel a little less . . . weird, I guess, since I often struggle with doubt too.

In John 14, Jesus had been teaching His disciples about the Father. Some of the concepts weren't sticking with Philip (maybe similar to me and math). So "Philip said, 'Lord, show us the Father and that will be enough for us'" (v. 8). Philip seemed to be looking for sensory proof, similar to the way Thomas wanted to touch Jesus's scars after His resurrection.

What a beautiful gift Jesus gave us when He answered Philip: "Anyone who has seen me has seen the Father" (v. 9). This helps us in our quest to know God. We can simply look at Jesus. We can study who Jesus was when He walked the earth. We can look at the things He did, the stories He told, and the people He spent time with. When we know Jesus, we know the Father.

Experiencing Father God's Protection

Looking at Jesus's life is one way we can get to know our Father. Can you think of a trait Jesus showed that helps you understand who God is? List it here: _____.

Now thank your Father for that trait: Father, thank You that Jesus is _____ (fill in the blank with the trait you thought of). I am very glad that I can read about who Jesus is so I can understand who You are. In Jesus's name, amen.

Growing Stronger

Read John 11:38–44. In the lines below, list the traits you see in Jesus that show us what the Father is like.

_____

_____

_____

_____

_____

_____

_____

_____

_____

_____

_____

_____

_____

3

Jesus Prayed for Our Protection

MICHELLE

"I will remain in the world no longer, but they are still in the world, and I am coming to you. Holy Father, protect them by the power of your name, the name you gave me, so that they may be one as we are one."

JOHN 17:11

Even though I'm an extrovert, walking into a crowded room with lots of people I don't know still makes me nervous. I feel vulnerable because I don't know what they will think of me. I wonder how we will interact. However, I feel better when I have a friend with me. Having someone I know and trust helps me feel more protected. Having someone beside me makes me feel like they will have my back and make the situation less awkward, especially if something goes wrong.

Jesus prayed for us, knowing we'd need heavenly support in situations like these. When we feel we are at our weakest, we can rely on the power of God, which covers us through the Father's name—our connection to Him. If our Father has the power to move mountains (Job 9:5), His power can give us the confidence we need to interact with new people.

What if the next time you worried about not being liked—or worse, being rejected—you realized that you are never alone? Father God is with you, and He can be your protector. Learning to lean on and trust in His protection isn't easy. Many of us like to be independent and have learned to lean only on our own strength. We also have learned to see this world only through human eyes, which leads us to focus on what we can see. But as we recognize God's presence with us, we can train our spirits to focus on the unseen (2 Corinthians 4:18).

Experiencing Father God's Protection

God, help me trust You to protect me when I feel like I just can't _____(fill in the blank with your own anxious situation). As I navigate this world that seems so hard at times, I know I can learn to experience the power of Your name. Amen.

Growing Stronger

Read 2 Corinthians 4:18. Make a list of unseen things—like God's love, angels watching over you, or even moments of past successes—that you can focus on the next time you encounter a situation that makes you feel insecure.

4

Abba Leads Me

LYNN

"I led them with cords of human kindness, with ties of love. To them I was like one who lifts a little child to the cheek, and I bent down to feed them."

HOSEA 11:4

When I was a teen, there were things about God I understood. Or at least I thought I did. I understood God sent His perfect Son into the world to die for my sins because He loved me. I understood Jesus was that Son, the One who took on my sin, giving me a new life to live for Him. My understanding stopped there though. My heart didn't comprehend the depth of that love.

I now see that I had a gap of understanding between my head and heart. I've heard this called "the difficult twelve inches from the head to the heart"; the twelve inches that makes all the difference.

Like my relationship with God, I knew my dad loved me. Like my experience with God, he proved it by providing for me. Unlike God, though, my dad was quiet. His dad died when he was young, creating a gap of sorts in his heart, like I had in mine. I think this is why conversations with my dad were few. Expressing love with words, emotions, or hugs was uncomfortable for him. I was twenty-one years old when I heard Dad say for the first time, "I love you too." And kisses? I remember one for a picture on my wedding day.

I have often felt sad that my relationship with my dad had gaps in it from unspoken words and expressions of love. I desperately tried to fill this gap with approval from other people. With the help of some who understood the Father heart of God, I began to see Father God as engaging, loving, compassionate, merciful, and affectionate.

Hosea 11:4 drew a picture I had never seen: "I led them with cords of human kindness, with ties of love. To them I was like one who lifts a little child to the cheek, and I bent down to feed them." My heart could hardly believe *this* is what Father God was like. Lifting me to His cheek? This Father wanted a kiss from me. He wants this interactive love with you too!

Experiencing Father God's Protection

When my child was a toddler, he wanted to be independent. He would run off, often into potentially dangerous situations. Your parent or caregiver might have had this experience too. In order to keep you safe, they may have used a teddy bear backpack with a leash on it, a sort of tie of love. This tie of love kept you near and safe. Father God also wants to protect you because He loves you dearly. How might you see Father God's protection in your life?

Growing Stronger

Read Hosea 11. What other ways do you see our relationship with Father God being compared to that of a human parent and child? Share in the lines below.

5

From the Evil One

MICHELLE

"My prayer is not that you take them out of the
world but that you protect them from the evil one."

JOHN 17:15

Because we tend to focus on things we can see, we forget there is an evil one on earth that wants to steal, kill, and destroy (John 10:10). Have you ever had a time in your life when you felt like nothing was going right? That's been my life lately as I've experienced several injuries and can't do what I usually do. Because I'm dealing with physical pain, I'm not enjoying anything as much as I used to. I want to go out with friends and have fun, but when I do, I end up exhausted and it almost doesn't seem worth it.

Have you ever felt like this? Had days when it feels easier to stay in your room, under the covers, maybe even with just a pet for company? It's easy in times like these to begin to feel so stuck—so stuck that our doing nothing leads to having even less energy, so that things we once enjoyed seem draining.

We have to be careful of getting stuck in feelings like these, because the Evil One loves to discourage God's people. It's a battle to not give in and give up.

Jesus didn't pray that we would be delivered from all the suffering we experience as humans on earth, but He did ask God to protect us from the Evil One. Recently, I've been claiming promises for God's protection over my life. When we sense Father God's protection, we begin to feel the darkness go away because we know the light of God can overcome our darkness (John 1:5).

Experiencing Father God's Protection

As you claim God's protection from the Evil One, do one thing that will bring His light into your space. Open your blinds and curtains, then look outside at all He's created. Go for a walk and breathe in fresh air. Read or listen to a verse in the Bible. Listen to a song that reminds you of God's love, power, and truth. Talk to someone who knows God about how stuck you've been feeling.

Growing Stronger

Read Ephesians 6:10–18. Envision yourself putting on the full armor of God to protect you from your true enemy.

6

Can You See It?

For since the creation of the world God's invisible qualities—his eternal power and divine nature—have been clearly seen, being understood from what has been made, so that people are without excuse.

ROMANS 1:20

When I drive in the mountains, tears well up in my eyes. The beautiful blue ridges seem to go on forever. Paul—the author of the book of Romans, where today's verse is found—wrote that creation gives us a picture of who our Father is. When we see creation, we see His power. When we experience the sun rising and setting each and every day, we know His faithfulness. What a kind, good Father we have to make such beauty to show us who He is!

As I write, I'm looking out my window and I see a deer. A strong creature, it strides across our lawn, heading to the shade of the trees to get out of the heat.

When I see beautiful animals like this, the mountains, a flower in a field, a shell washed up on the sand, or the colored leaves drifting from trees in the fall, I think of how much our Father loves us. He didn't *need* to make such beauty. Our entire world could be khaki, tan, and taupe with no colorful dimension.

He didn't have to create stunning sea life below the surface of the ocean. Such artistry speaks of His greatness. Through His creation He says to us, *See what I made! All for you! Do you see Me?*

Sometimes, when I'm considering buying flowers for myself, I think, *That's not necessary.* Yet, neither was it necessary for our Father to design flowers in so many different elegant and complex ways that give us enjoyment. He did, whispering love for you and me with the extravagance of His creation.

This is the type of love our Father has for you and me. It's not only practical, logical, or useful. Sometimes it also shows His love in ways that are more than necessary just so we know how much we are adored!

Experiencing Father God's Protection

One way our Father protects us is through His creation. Getting outdoors promotes good mental health, boosting our growth and healing. Get outside today and allow the sunshine to bring vitamin D to you, a hormone that helps support our overall physical and mental well-being. Look for something your Father has created and thank Him for loving you this way.

Growing Stronger

Plan some time in the near future to get outside and spend a longer length of time with your Father. Take your Bible and a journal. Read Job 12:7–10 and write out how you see your Father in His creation.

1

God to the Rescue

MICHELLE

"Because he loves me," says the LORD, "I
will rescue him; I will protect him, for he
acknowledges my name."

PSALM 91:14

Have you ever not wanted your life because things weren't going the way you'd hoped? Or wished your life was like a story in a book where you could choose a different ending? I've talked with many girls who have. They feel like nothing good is happening in their lives. Many would like to go back and change choices they've made. Some wish that they could wave a magic wand and escape all the pressure they feel.

Our Father loves us so much that He wants us to turn to Him to be our rescuer instead of trying to escape. I can remember times I've made a bad mistake and prayed hard that things would all work out. Sometimes the situations got worse before they got better, but whenever I've turned to God, I've felt His presence. In a world that teaches us "we are enough," being able to turn to Him helps us know it's not only up to us, which provides relief and a sense of not being alone. If we miss asking God for help in our lives, we miss the opportunity to be aware of how He can work all things—even mistakes—for our good (Romans 8:28).

Sometimes when we pray, God doesn't change our circumstances, but we can sense His presence and protection as we walk through difficult times. Father God wants to be included in our lives, especially when we need His help. He even sent the Holy Spirit, a permanent helper to live inside us and always be with us, empowering us to face hard times with a confidence we could never imagine with only our own strength.

Experiencing Father God's Protection

Father, thank You for wanting to be my Rescuer and Protector. I need You and want to turn to You when I need help. Right now, will You help me with _____? Thank You for listening to me and loving me. Give me strength to do what needs to be done today. I'm so glad I'm Your child, today and always.

Growing Stronger

Read John 14:15–17. Thank God for sending you the Holy Spirit. Invite the Holy Spirit to be your helper.

8

Never Too Busy

LYNN

And he took the children in his arms, placed his
hands on them and blessed them.

MARK 10:16

When my children were little, I was always moving: getting them to school, taking them to activities, putting in laundry, going grocery shopping, and doing all the things we needed to keep our busy lives rolling. I've discovered that once you get used to being busy, it can almost become addictive.

In Mark 10:13–16, it is clear that Jesus sees us as more than simply what we do, more valuable than our performance:

> People were bringing little children to Jesus for him to place his hands on them, but the disciples rebuked them. When Jesus saw this, he was indignant. He said to them, "Let the little children come to me, and do not hinder them, for the kingdom of God belongs to such as these. Truly I tell you, anyone who will not receive the kingdom of God like a little child will never enter it." And he took the children in his arms, placed his hands on them and blessed them.

As little children crawled into Jesus's lap, His disciples got mad. Possibly thinking Jesus didn't have time or want to be bothered, the disciples scolded those bringing their children. The NIV translation says Jesus was "indignant," but the meaning in the original Greek (which this part of the Bible was written in) is closer to the word **grieving.**[*]

Yes, Jesus was mad that the little ones were being turned away, but it also made Him sad. He didn't want children to get the impression that He was too busy for them. He didn't want them to think they were not loved or important. Children tend to play and make messes without being productive. Jesus loved them as they were. He took them into His arms. Can't you see Him giving them a bear hug, their heads resting on His chest next to His heart? He showed them the love of Father God.

This picture of our Father is causing tears to pool in my eyes. I hope like me, you see the gentle, caring heart of God. He's not too busy for you! He's not annoyed or bothered by you . . . ever! Instead, His arms are open wide as He says, *Come! Crawl up on My lap and let Me hold you.*

Experiencing Father God's Protection

Maybe you've believed the lie that Father God doesn't want to be bothered or doesn't have time for your "petty" emotions or troubles. It's not true. Satan puts these thoughts in our minds to keep us from our Father. Shut your eyes and picture your little-person self climbing up into the lap of Father God as He draws you close to His heart.

Growing Stronger

Read Isaiah 40:11. What picture do you see here? Draw it on a separate piece of paper or describe in the space below.

_____

_____

_____

---

[*] *Strong's Concordance*, s.v. "aganakteó (v.)," accessed March 22, 2024, https://biblehub.com/greek/23.htm.

9

God's Gift of Fear

MICHELLE

*Some trust in chariots and some in horses, but
we trust in the name of the LORD our God. They
are brought to their knees and fall, but we rise up
and stand firm.*

PSALM 20:1-8

When I was a student at Baylor University, we had to attend special trainings in our dorm because Waco had an active rapist on the loose, and he was attacking women in the campus parking lots. They encouraged us to never go to our cars or walk to the dorm at night unescorted. At first, I was annoyed because I felt invincible and indestructible. Like many young people, I believed I was the exception to the rule and nothing bad would happen to me. Maybe you've felt that way before too, like when driving a car a little too fast or taking a dare that seemed risky to others. On campus, the self-defense expert emphasized we needed to be constantly aware of our surroundings. I thought about how I'd learned in Bible class that God is omnipresent—with us everywhere all the time. He is also omniscient, which means He's all-knowing. Sitting in the lobby of the girls' dorm that night, I prayed, *Father, You are my protector. Help me to be wise and alert as I enjoy college life. I don't want to live in fear, but I do want to tap into Your presence. When danger is near, help me recognize the threat and trust my instincts.* After praying, I no longer felt as annoyed that I couldn't go out alone, because I knew being in groups was part of God's protection for me.

Experiencing Father God's Protection

As you move around the area where you live—go to school, work, and spend your time—whether in a vehicle or other mode of transportation, take a moment to thank God for His protection. Ask your heavenly Father to help you be alert, make wise decisions about who you trust, and guide you to safety when danger is near.

Growing Stronger

Choose a verse or phrase that you can repeat when you need God's protection or when you feel like you might be in danger. I like Psalm 46:1: "God is our refuge and strength, always ready to help in times of trouble" (NLT). Write the phrase/verse on the lines below.

10

Welcome Home!

LYNN

Then God said, "Let us make human beings in our image, to be like us. They will reign over the fish in the sea, the birds in the sky, the livestock, all the wild animals on the earth, and the small animals that scurry along the ground."

GENESIS 1:26 NLT

Have you ever tried painting, pottery, or another type of artistic expression? Our family has been to a pottery studio, where we painted vases, tiles, and other ceramic pieces. The studios have samples to copy, but the pieces that are the most special are our original designs.

That is what you are! Your Father's original design. Genesis 1:27 tells us God created you and me in His image. We were made to reflect the likeness and character of our Father and represent Him to our world. This was the beginning of our story as His child; it began with our Father.

From the very first chapter of the very first book of the Bible, we get a glimpse into who our Father is. He is the Creator, the One who has the power to make something out of nothing.

He is Maker, creating the sun to govern by day and the moon to rule by night. He is Provider, creating food for us before He even created us.

We also see the perfect family of the Trinity. They were all there at creation: Father, Son, and Spirit. The Trinity is the "us" written about in Genesis 1:26 when the author wrote, "Then God said, 'Let us make human beings in our image, to be like us'" (NLT).

From the beginning, we were created to look like our Father. When we know who our Father is, we will know who we are.

Experiencing Father God's Protection

How would you describe yourself?

_____

_____

_____

How do these traits you wrote about yourself align with what you know about Father God?

_____

_____

_____

One way your Father wants to protect you is by helping you see yourself accurately. If you struggled to write things above about what you and God share, or if the things you feel about yourself and what you know to be true about God do not match, remember that you were created in His image when He formed you in your mother's womb. Ask Father God to begin to change the way you see yourself and to begin to see yourself as being more like your Father.

Growing Stronger

Read Psalm 8:5 and Psalm 100:3. In the space below, write some of the ways the psalmist describes us in these verses.

_____

_____

_____

_____

_____

11

A Barricade for the Beloved

LYNN

So the LORD God banished him from the Garden of Eden to work the ground from which he had been taken.

GENESIS 3:23

There have been times in my life when Father God created opportunities for me that I never dreamed would occur. Books I got to write. Trips I was asked to take. Groups I was able to join. Other times He lovingly closed the door on opportunities I assumed He would open. He closed the door even though I *knew* (in other words, thought) these opportunities were His best for me. In actuality, they weren't.

When Father God opened doors and shut others, He demonstrated His love. He proved Himself faithful, even during times when I desired experiences that would have not been for my good or when I didn't want the protection He was providing.

Father God performed an action in the story of Adam and Eve (Genesis 3) that can feel confusing. After Eve sinned, Father God sent Adam and Eve *out* of beautiful Eden.

When my young brain read this story, I thought: *How mean! They made a mistake and now they'll be punished forever?* I had no idea how great Father God's love was for Adam and Eve and every one of their descendants, which includes all of us. After sin entered the earth, the garden was no longer safe; it became dangerous. Once sin entered the earth, the human body began to age and eventually decay. If Adam and

Eve ate from the Tree of Life, they would live forever in those decaying bodies (Genesis 3:22). Can you imagine living forever in a body that was broken, sick, and frail? God made sure this would not happen; He set a boundary protecting them and every human ever to exist.

Maybe as Adam and Eve stood outside of the garden, they felt confused by the cherubim and the flaming sword keeping them out (Genesis 3:24). *Why would our Father do this?* they may have thought.

Father God was loving His children by keeping them from what they didn't have the power or wisdom to keep away from themselves.

Experiencing Father God's Protection

Recall a time you wanted something, you didn't get it, and you later discovered it wasn't for your best. Write out a prayer of thanks below.

Here is an example to help you get started if you'd like one: Father God, thank You for protecting us from ourselves. Thank You for placing barricades in our path when we haven't had the knowledge or wisdom we needed. Thank You for keeping us from what appears desirable but isn't good for us. In Jesus's name, amen.

Growing Stronger

The Bible uses the metaphor of a door many times. Look up two or three of these verses: Matthew 7:7, John 10:9, Acts 14:27, and Revelation 3:8. In each verse, what type of door is being described?

12

When We Long for Love

MICHELLE

Above all else, guard your heart, for everything you do flows from it.

PROVERBS 4:23

He's so perfect for me, even though he doesn't know God. He's better than most of the Christian guys I've been around. I know I'm not supposed to be dating him, but it just feels so right."

I've heard these words countless times from women sitting in front of me in the counseling office or at churches where I've led small groups. Waiting on the right guy is hard. I get it because I didn't get married until I was thirty-two. Some years I was busy and enjoyed being single, but other years were really hard. I thought I'd be married by twenty-five and start a family soon after because I loved kids. Turning thirty was painful since the number of single guys at church was getting smaller and smaller. (There seemed to be three girls to every one guy.)

During those lonely days when everyone, including my sisters, was getting engaged and married, I remember thinking that maybe my standards were too high. Maybe I shouldn't care as much about marrying a godly man. Maybe I should settle for a good guy. Then I became a counselor at twenty-seven and a marriage counselor before I was thirty. Seeing broken marriages and women struggling in their relationships where their partner didn't share their faith changed my view and encouraged me to keep waiting.

Since then, I've walked beside many women during their painful breakups. Some breakups occurred because they chose God over continuing to date someone they had a lot in common with but who lacked a commitment to pursue God wholeheartedly. Many happened when they caught their boyfriend or fiancé cheating on them. These godly women chose to experience the pain of current loss to avoid future misery.

Experiencing Father God's Protection

Whether you are just starting to look at the possibility of dating or have been dating for a long time, ask God to help you make wise choices when your heart starts beating fast and you get those wonderful butterflies in your stomach. Seek His strength when you need to resist temptation and attraction to a guy you know won't be good for you in the long run.

Growing Stronger

When I taught the book *Boundaries in Dating*, I made a list of characteristics I wanted in the men I dated. I even made a list of nonnegotiables like *loves God*, *admits his mistakes*, and *values family*. I encourage you to work on a list for yourself if you don't already have one, or, if you do, to take another look at it. Also make sure the list doesn't contain a lot of superficial characteristics and is realistic (no man is perfect!), so you're not overlooking someone who could be a great match simply because he has average looks or isn't planning to make a lot of money.

13

You Surround Me

LYNN

For in the day of trouble he will keep me safe in his dwelling; he will hide me in the shelter of his sacred tent and set me high upon a rock.

PSALM 27:5

Excited to visit her friend, our daughter sang her heart out while heading down the highway on a solo trip. Suddenly, she spotted a large SUV parked on the shoulder, beginning to make its way back onto the road. The SUV was attempting to do a U-turn in the middle of the interstate! There was no way it would make it! She gasped in fear, realizing a crash was coming. Within seconds, our daughter's compact car smashed into the side of the turning SUV, crushing her car and forcing the SUV to flip.

Trapped in her vehicle, our daughter pushed on her bashed-in door with all her might, releasing herself from her totaled car. As she examined her injuries, she almost couldn't believe what she discovered. Looking at her body, she saw she was whole and safe. Later, as we looked at the mangled car, we saw a pocket of protection Father God had provided, holding her close in her day of trouble.

In Psalm 27:5, David spoke of this type of protection: "For in the day of trouble he will keep me safe in his dwelling; he will hide me in the shelter of his sacred tent and set me high upon a rock." I love that David said "he will" two times. David was looking to the future and reminding himself God will protect him.

You and I have no idea what this day will hold. As children of God, we are not exempt from pain and hardship—in fact, Jesus warned we'd face struggles in life (John 16:33). But the Bible also promises we can trust that no matter what comes, our Father sees it and will help us through. God was with my daughter; and just as David knew God would be with him, God is with us. Father God's protection surrounds us.

Experiencing Father God's Protection

Close your eyes and picture yourself safe in God's dwelling, hiding in God's tent. You are set high upon a rock or mountain, safe in God's care. Thank Him for protecting you today, in His wisdom, in His way.

Growing Stronger

Read Psalm 91 out loud, making it your prayer.

14

Broken Up but Not Broken

MICHELLE

"For I know the plans I have for you," declares the Lord, *"plans to prosper you and not to harm you, plans to give you hope and a future."*

JEREMIAH 29:11

When I was thirty years old, long before dating apps, I met a man at a Christian dating event. He approached me at the end of my training for singles and asked me out for coffee. Long story short, that night turned into many dates, but he told me he loved me right away. His quick declaration concerned me because I believed love was more than just a feeling; it was a choice and a commitment. Just as quickly as his feeling came, it seemed to disappear in a matter of months. As we traveled overseas so he could meet my parents—who were missionaries—I realized this relationship would soon end. Anxiety from wanting to hold on propelled me to try harder, but in my heart, I knew my prayers for love and marriage would once again be a no-go. The night we broke up I felt devastated. I couldn't sleep or eat. I experienced physical pain in my chest.

This man and I had planned to get engaged on Valentine's Day, but instead I ran into an ex-boyfriend, Drew, at a mutual friend's wedding. He congratulated me, as he had heard I was getting married. Avoiding his eyes so he wouldn't see my grief, I quickly let him know we had broken up. Drew later told me he celebrated in his mind with a big *Yes!*

as he outwardly, kindly expressed sympathy that it didn't work out. Drew also began planning his pursuit. Today, we've been mostly happily married for over twenty years. I thank Father God for His protection from the marriage I thought I wanted because I'm now grateful for the one I have.

Experiencing Father God's Protection

Think of a time when God said no to a prayer request and that ended up being a good thing. Maybe it was trying out for a play or a sports team, wanting to date a guy you later discovered was a player, or getting rejected from a college that you later found out wouldn't have been the place for you. Thank your heavenly Father for His protection, and ask Him to help you trust Him even when you want something really bad.

Growing Stronger

My family and coworkers gave me great support when my relationship ended. Ask other girls and guys about a time they experienced God's no: How did they manage the hard moments? What did He teach them while they were suffering?

15

I've Got It

LYNN

But you, God, see the trouble of the afflicted;
you consider their grief and take it in hand. The
victims commit themselves to you; you are the
helper of the fatherless.

PSALM 10:14

Walking through the front door, my child shared through tears another story of bullying on the bus. I just couldn't take it anymore. The cruel words were tearing up her heart and mine. Yet when I spoke of going to the principal to get this trouble resolved, she cried, "No!" Whether from embarrassment or fear of even more bullying, she did not want me involved. She wanted to handle it on her own.

You and I might also desire independence from our Father God and attempt to handle situations or struggles on our own. When we choose this path, we don't take our troubles to the One who can help us. We don't depend on Him to come and protect us. Yet Psalm 10 tells us God sees our hardships, considers our grief, and will "take it in hand." In another translation, it says, "The helpless put their trust in you. You defend the orphans" (NLT).

God knows your problems; He is not absent, nor does He want to be an uninvolved parent. In fact, He is "the helper of the fatherless." Will you put your trust in Him to help you? Will you choose to commit yourself to "the helper to the fatherless"? He is watching you wrestle, waiting for you to come to Him so He can protect you. At times the assistance He provides may not be exactly what we want. Yet, as we

PROTECTOR

32

practice trusting Father God, we will get more comfortable depending on Him for the protection we need.

Experiencing Father God's Protection

Are you experiencing trouble that is overwhelming you? What would it look like to have your Father "take it in hand" today? In the space below, write how you can choose to trust Him to help you in the middle of your trouble.

Growing Stronger

Read Psalm 10:14, Psalm 50:15, and Psalm 59:16–17. Create or locate a graphic on at least one of the verses and share it with a friend who is currently feeling defeated.

16

God's Discipline as Prevention

MICHELLE

We do not enjoy being disciplined. It is painful at the time, but later, after we have learned from it, we have peace, because we start living in the right way.

HEBREWS 12:11 NCV

I love being busy. I like being recognized and admired for my hard work, but I can get carried away to the point it takes a toll on my mental, physical, and spiritual health.

As a high school senior, my overcommitted self went into overdrive. During an important tennis match, I injured my left hip and wrist. My doctor said finishing the season was out of the question. Though I felt like all my dreams of a partial tennis scholarship were dying, I gained a slower, better pace in life.

Earthly fathers can dole out harsh punishment. I've heard too many stories of paddles and belt buckles that left marks and faces being slapped. But our heavenly Father's discipline is different. It ends with a greater purpose. My daughter, while driving on the highway, groans when she encounters barrier walls. They put her entire body on alert. But they serve a greater purpose—to make us reduce our speed so we will be safe.

Slowing down is a lesson in discipline I've had to keep repeating because I struggle to say no. These past few years, in the midst of running the counseling center, traveling and speaking around the country, and writing and promoting books, I needed several major surgeries. Also, my dad was diagnosed with cancer and died in less than a month. I even experienced an emergency hospitalization due to internal bleeding. These events resulted in months of crucial downtime while I recovered.

I'm growing stronger through physical therapy, and I have lots of energy after so much rest. I can see now that if I had kept the pace I was on, I might have experienced a breakdown. My medical downtimes and grief allowed me to not only recover physically but also rediscover a healthier pace in which to run my race (Hebrews 12:1).

Experiencing Father God's Protection

Bad things happen, but our Father can use them for good when we seek His help (Romans 8:28). If you're going through a hard time right now, ask Father God to help you create changes that can make it easier to suffer through it well. If you made some poor choices that partially led to your struggle, ask your Father for forgiveness, receiving it as He welcomes your repentance with His embrace.

Growing Stronger

Meditate on this verse from Scripture: "Cease striving and know that I am God" (Psalm 46:10 NASB). Ask your Father to show you areas in your life that are making you too busy to be healthy. Ask for the strength to make some difficult decisions, even if it means giving up amazing opportunities, trusting that God will provide them again when you have more bandwidth.

17

Is That You, Father?

LYNN

*He reached down from on high and took hold of
me; he drew me out of deep waters.
He rescued me from my powerful enemy, from my
foes, who were too strong for me.*

PSALM 18:16–17

Our vacation plans were perfect! A local had provided a crowd-free recommendation for a natural waterslide on the side of a mountain. We were ready for adventure!

Our older children scrambled up, slid down, and screamed before hitting the water. How fun! Our youngest prepared to slide next. Suddenly, I sensed a still, small voice I'd come to recognize as the voice of our heavenly Father, warning me that since she was smaller and weighed less, she shouldn't go alone. Yelling at her to wait, I asked Greg, her dad, to slide with her. Putting her on his lap, he gave a push. As they slid down the granite, they began sliding crooked, heading right for the rock face! Sticking out his leg so the rock hit his leg instead of their heads, they spun around. Greg's back slammed into the jagged mountain, preventing them from serious injury.

If they had hit their heads on the rock, the injury could've been traumatic. Instead, Father God protected them with His prompting, and we cooperated through our obedience.

With time and practice, you can learn to listen and hear the protective voice of Father God. He chooses to protect us by giving us warnings, like the warning I experienced before our child went down the slippery rock. Listening to and heeding the Father's voice can save us from some of the trouble the Enemy puts in our paths.

Sometimes Father God's voice can feel like a hesitation, prompting us to take a second look at a choice we were going to make. We can ask ourselves: *Is this best for me?* Other times His voice may feel like excitement, encouraging us with the awareness God is opening a new opportunity for us. The more we listen and follow His voice, the more we will recognize it.

Experiencing Father God's Protection

You can hear your heavenly Father's voice. He wants you to! If you have a decision you need to make, ask Him to speak to you and then begin to anticipate He will supply the answer. At first, you may not feel that your heavenly Father is speaking. I can still struggle with hearing Him even after listening and talking to Father God for years. Don't give up. Keep asking, keep seeking, and trust that in time you will recognize His voice.

Growing Stronger

Read John 10. List some of the interactions between us as sheep and Jesus our Shepherd on the lines below.

_____

_____

_____

_____

_____

18

Creating a Safe Place with God

MICHELLE

You are my hiding place; you will protect me from trouble and surround me with songs of deliverance.

PSALM 32:1

When a client struggles with anxiety or wants to heal from trauma, one of the first exercises we teach in our offices is Safe Place. We ask them to pick a place that they've been or imagined where they felt totally safe. Next, we involve their senses by asking them to describe everything they can see when in that place. Many people choose the beach. They describe the way the sun sparkles on the waves and how the water ripples around their feet. We ask them to share with us what they hear. They talk about the sound of the waves, a breeze, or a seagull. We then ask them to describe what they feel, and they tell us about the hot sand or cool water. We even ask them to bring to mind what they can smell and taste.

Next, we ask them to identify the positive feelings in their body. Often their chest feels lighter and their muscles more relaxed.

The last step is to pair a word that describes what they're feeling with the positive emotions and experiences the safe place created. We often use words like **calm**, **peaceful**, and **relaxed**.

Lastly, if the client is a Christ follower, I then ask them if it feels okay to bring God into their safe place. I remind them that He desires to be a hiding place for us from the troubles of the world.

I hope you will take this exercise and practice it when you need a sense of calm and safety in our broken world. Father God is our Creator and He made safe surroundings for us to enjoy. When He and His creation become part of our safe place, we can find peace no matter where we are.

Experiencing Father God's Protection

Create a safe place in your mind that you can "go to" anytime you feel overwhelmed. Use all of your senses as you imagine it. As you take a reality break, breathe in as you count to three and then out as you count to three. Feel your breath connect with your Creator, who breathed the breath of life into you (Genesis 2:7).

Growing Stronger

Practice "going" to your safe place in your mind even when you don't need its comfort. Consider the exercise a preemptive strike. Dwelling there with God creates a sense of calm in your life that will be easier to access when life's challenges invade your peace.

19

Tattooing the Father's Word

LYNN

Blessed are you, Israel! Who is like you, a people saved by the LORD? He is your shield and helper and your glorious sword. Your enemies will cower before you, and you will tread on their heights.

DEUTERONOMY 33:29

Could other people see my lip quivering? Maybe I should pop into the bathroom and look?

It was my first day of high school and I was transferring from a Christian school to a public school. I felt God wanted me to change schools so I could be a light for Him, but that didn't mean I wasn't scared.

That first year of high school was very hard. I felt invisible walking down the halls, trying to find friends, and looking for spaces where I belonged.

As lonely as some days were, I knew I wasn't alone. By taping verses inside my locker door, I reminded myself: God is my helper. He is with me.

Personalizing verses by putting *my* name in them helped me to "tattoo" them in my mind. This practice reminded me that the character qualities Father God exemplified to His people, He wanted me to exemplify to others. Not all verses in the Bible are promises, nor are all promises given directly to us, but they are principles displaying God's character.

Deuteronomy 33:29 speaks of a physical enemy of God's people, the Israelites. The Enemy we experience is often not a physical enemy, such as a person, but an enemy of our soul. This Enemy wants to drag us back to our hurts, throw us in a cell called **failure**, and throw away the key. But God is always ready to help us! Father God stands for us and is trustworthy. He is our helper (Psalm 10:14). He helps and empowers us to stand in hard situations. We are held by Father God. He picks us up and we stand on His strength.

Experiencing Father God's Protection

Try the practice of putting your name in a verse by using the one at the beginning of this devotion. I have done it here with my name: "Blessed are you, Lynn! Who is like you, Lynn, saved by the LORD? He is my shield and helper and my glorious sword. My enemies will cower before me and I will tread on their heights. He is my beautiful weapon to fight my enemy of fear, sadness, loneliness, abandonment, betrayal, and comparison."

Growing Stronger

Choose one of the following passages: Psalm 10:14, Psalm 18:16–17, or Psalm 27:5. Replace the appropriate pronouns with your name and enter the verse in your phone or write it on a piece of paper that you can look at throughout the day today.

20

Protection from Perfection and Procrastination

MICHELLE

Rescue me from my enemies, O God. Protect me from those who have come to destroy me.

PSALM 59:1 NLT

The Israelites had enemies they could see. Most people I work with battle unseen enemies. These enemies bear names like **procrastination, perfectionism, self-doubt,** and **fear of failure.** Although not physically surrounding us, they lead to lives that get stuck or stop working. These enemies cause us to withdraw from the very tasks God has called us to complete.

Abba Father provides a way for us to be rescued from the invisible foes that lead to self-sabotage. **Grace** is a five-letter word with the power to free us from the need to never fail. When we apply grace to our guilt—and even our shame—we can begin that work we've been avoiding. Grace applied to perfectionism makes getting a grade of less than 100 more tolerable.

When we give ourselves permission to just do the best we can in any moment in time, we can talk our way toward beginning something that appears too difficult and demands what seems like more energy than we feel we can exert. Accepting that our human efforts are good enough for Father God is often the first step. The next is to accept that our efforts are good enough for us too. Allowing ourselves to be human empowers us to study and do the best we can. Giving ourselves grace can even help us fill a blank screen with words for that overdue assignment. When life's demands come fast and furious, doing our best with God's help is all that we can do, and it can be enough if we let it.

Experiencing Father God's Protection

Identify one or two tasks you've been avoiding. Now imagine yourself doing them with grace, which allows you to stumble and maybe not do the best you've ever done but still get the task done.

Growing Stronger

Dwell on these words from the chorus of "Grace Greater Than All Our Sin." Let His grace cleanse you today so you can start again.

Grace, grace, God's grace,
Grace that will pardon and cleanse within;
Grace, grace, God's grace,
Grace that is greater than all our sin.*

---

* "Grace Greater Than All Our Sin," words by Julia H. Johnston and music by Daniel B. Towner, public domain.

Healer

MEDITATION MATTERS

For as high as the heavens are above the earth, so great is his love for those who fear him; as far as the east is from the west, so far has he removed our transgressions from us.

PSALM 103:11–12

Praise be to the God and Father of our Lord Jesus Christ, the Father of compassion and the God of all comfort, who comforts us in all our troubles, so that we can comfort those in any trouble with the comfort we ourselves receive from God.

2 CORINTHIANS 1:3–4

As a father has compassion on his children, so the Lord has compassion on those who fear him; for he knows how we are formed, he remembers that we are dust.

PSALM 103:13–14

You keep track of all my sorrows. You have collected all my tears in your bottle. You have recorded each one in your book.

PSALM 56:8 NLT

1

A Root of the Hurt

LYNN

Cleanse me with hyssop, and I will be clean; wash me, and I will be whiter than snow.

PSALM 51:7

Why is it that sometimes those I love and who also love me seem to have the greatest power to hurt me?

When this happened in my life recently, the more I dwelt on what happened, the more I wanted to point my finger at the other person. *It was their fault!* I reasoned. I wasn't really open to hearing God's perspective on the situation. My pride, as it always does, didn't want me to see *my* part in the problem.

Days passed. The next thing I knew, a week had gone by and I was still struggling to acknowledge my part. Hurtful words replayed in my mind when I woke up, during the day at work, and at night as I struggled to sleep. I needed to admit my part, my sin, in the situation. If I didn't, bitterness was going to set in.

What do we do when we're wrestling with heart wounds and wanting to be healed?

It starts with confessing our sin to God if we have played any part in the hurtful situation. David described it this way in Psalm 51:4: "Against you, you only, have I sinned and done what is evil in your sight." We may have sinned against another person, but the first person we need to ask forgiveness from is God. This is called **confession**. When we confess our sins, the cleansing of our wound begins. David went on to pray: "Cleanse me with hyssop, and I will be clean; wash me, and I will be whiter than snow" (v. 7). This is what we want: to be made right with God and to have our hearts made whole again.

Experiencing Father God's Healing

Do you have a wound—either old or new—that needs God's healing? Take a moment to ask your Father to reveal any part you may have played in the situation. If He shows you something, ask Him to forgive you and wash your heart clean. If you are blameless, pray that God will help you heal from someone else's choices in our broken world. Receive what you need from Him and thank your heavenly Father that you are always forgiven because of His Son, Jesus.

Growing Stronger

Read all of Psalm 51. What heart changes or actions do you want to implement after reading this devotional? Is there someone you need to reach out to and ask for their forgiveness?

2

Betrayed but Not Forgotten

MICHELLE

He heals the brokenhearted and binds up their wounds.

PSALM 147:3

I can't believe she isn't returning my calls or texts. And she's ignoring me at school. I thought we'd be best friends for the rest of our lives." I sat attentively listening as one of my clients poured out her heart to me, tears flowing down her face. Whether it's a close friend who finds a new bestie or the boy of their dreams who now likes someone else, many young women experience the intense pain of rejection and betrayal. They feel their hearts being torn apart and their futures forever changed. Dreams ended. Promises broken.

"No one understands how much it hurts," I often hear. When our pain is overwhelming, we feel that the hurt is so bad it will last forever. When we lose someone special in our lives, our pain begins a process of grief that takes time to walk through. We wish there was some way to get back what we had. Sometimes, we latch on to someone or something that will make it better fast. Immediate pain relief supersedes the wisdom of wise choices.

Think about a loving, wise parent you may have observed on a television show or witnessed in another family. Maybe you've wished you had someone in your life like that—and the truth is, you already do. Father God wants to comfort you in a similar way. He's well aware of all those thoughts in your head, where you replay what you could have done differently. He senses the deep hurt that makes you want to curl up in a ball on your bed. Abba Father longs to listen and, through His Spirit, provide words of comfort to ease your heartbreak.

Experiencing Father God's Healing

Has your heart been broken? It might have been in a romantic relationship, but not necessarily. Maybe you trusted someone you thought would be your best friend for life, but in time she chose a new friend or friends over you. Tell God about your pain, and let Him listen to your heart. Receive His healing. Let Him remind you that you are precious to Him.

Growing Stronger

Since life changes are inevitable, be prepared to make and keep three to four friends at any given time. Be assured that making new in-person friends is a process you will repeat often. Need a bigger friend circle? Introduce yourself to at least one new person this week. Start with small talk. Next, find a way to talk or text when you're not together. You could even take a giant leap of faith and ask them if they want to grab coffee or a snack.

3

Amazing and Wonderful

LYNN

I praise you because I am fearfully and
wonderfully made; your works are wonderful,
I know that full well.

PSALM 139:14

After waiting for what felt like forever, the special night at school arrived. For weeks, I had been creating combinations of outfits to wear for the big event, but I had never actually tried on my final choice. Now, as I stood in front of the full-length mirror, I got the full effect. It wasn't impressive. What I had seen in my mind was not the image before me. What I saw was boring and basic, at least in my eyes.

I wonder what would have happened if my dad were there that night. What if he had told me I was beautiful? What if he'd assured me there was more to me than my outfit? Maybe his reaction would have made a difference. I don't know because I don't have a memory of my dad from that important night in my life. As is true for many girls as they become women, my relationship with my dad was somewhat awkward.

Years later, someone shared with me today's verse, Psalm 139:14. I read this truth over and over and over . . . and I began to believe I was fearfully and wonderfully made. When the Father chose to create me, He took His time, making me into someone amazing and wonderful, not boring and basic. As I meditated on Father God's perspective of me, my perspective of myself began to align with His.

Experiencing Father God's Healing

Close your eyes and say to yourself, *Amazing and wonderful*, ten times. Today, every time you catch your reflection in a mirror, say to yourself: *Amazing and wonderful*. Write these words on a sticky note and place them on a mirror where you often check your appearance.

Growing Stronger

Using a Bible app or website such as BibleGateway.com or Biblehub .com, put in the verse Psalm 139:14 and read it in all of the English translations. Which version do you connect with the most?

4

God Will Restore

MICHELLE

"I will repay you for the years the locusts have eaten—the great locust and the young locust, the other locusts and the locust swarm—my great army that I sent among you."

JOEL 2:25

Even though I'm not a big fan of bugs, this Scripture about the locusts continues to be a promise I have claimed in my life when I feel like I'm losing too much. Since the people of God in the Old Testament counted on farming for their food, they dreaded these bugs because they destroy everything in their path.

Losing parts of our lives we love floods our bodies with painful grief. It's difficult to believe things will ever get better, especially when the bad days last weeks or months. Holding on to God's promise of being repaid for the years the locusts have taken is now something I cling to when my world falls apart.

When I was in my late twenties and did the right thing, I ended up losing my job. Since I was working for a church, I also lost some of my closest relationships as the congregation divided in two. Many from the counseling staff I supervised were evicted from the center I directed. A few weeks later, my boyfriend—the first man I'd ever loved—broke up with me. I thought I would never receive back all that had been taken, but over time, my Father restored it all. I had no idea that less than ten years later, I would have my own larger counseling center, lead and minister to others in a great church home, and that the boyfriend who broke up with me would become my husband.

Experiencing Father God's Healing

Is there something you've lost in your life that you'd like to see God restore? Ask Him to heal the brokenness inside your heart as you grieve and to restore in your life what was taken. You may have to give Him time to do so because the passage of time is an essential ingredient to the healing process. If you are like me, the waiting is hard. I'm horrible at it. Our Father's restoration may not look exactly how you expected. I've never held another church staff position since that season. What may have been one of your greatest losses could someday become one of your greatest testimonies of your heavenly Father's work in your life as your Healer and Restorer.

Growing Stronger

Read Philippians 3:8 and think of the greatness of gaining Christ in comparison to losing something important to you. Ask God to help you grieve well.

5

Cleansing, Healing Water

LYNN

On the last and greatest day of the festival, Jesus stood and said in a loud voice, "Let anyone who is thirsty come to me and drink. Whoever believes in me, as Scripture has said, rivers of living water will flow from within them."

JOHN 7:37–38

We were almost at the end of our five-mile hike; in fact, I could see the car. Suddenly, the rocks on the slope below my feet began to slide . . . and I slid right with them. My knee was the first to hit the gravel pathway. By the time I finished my tumble, I was all right, but I was dirty, shaken, and my knee was bleeding. After running to the car to get a cloth and water, my husband wiped the dirt from the wound. I cried as the icy water hit my fiery, burning skin. Yet my loving husband knew that if I was going to be healed, the cut had to be cleaned.

What is needed for our skinned knees is similar to what is needed for our wounded hearts. Before the medicine and adhesive strips are put on our hearts, dirt must be removed. The dirt can be pain-filled words spoken toward us, someone not doing what they said they would do, or any number of ways we've been disappointed and hurt by others. If these wounds are not "cleaned," a wall will begin to form around our hearts. These walls not only keep out the affections and care of others, they keep us far from the deep love of our heavenly Father. If you and

I are going to *fully* experience Father God's unconditional love, we're going to have to have our wounds cleaned first.

In John 7:37–38, Jesus refers to Himself as "living water." Jesus comes, with the Holy Spirit, as living water for our hearts so healing can begin. The healing He brings has an unlimited supply and is just what our hurting hearts need.

Sometimes when we anticipate the beginning of the healing process, we feel compelled to avoid opportunities to receive the restoration we need. Getting started can hurt, like the cold water on my burning knee. But if we are brave and let our heavenly Father's light and love penetrate our wound, we can experience the healing He wants to give us.

Experiencing Father God's Healing

Take a moment to pray and ask your Father to help you *want* to experience His healing. Here is a prayer prompt to get you started: Father God, ignoring painful things in my life seems easier than letting You treat them. Help me to be brave and allow You to begin the healing process of my heart. In Jesus's name, amen.

Growing Stronger

Read Psalm 103:1–5. What are the benefits of the Lord that the psalmist listed?

6

Faith for Healing

MICHELLE

Jesus turned and saw her. "Take heart,
daughter," he said, "your faith has healed you."
And the woman was healed at that moment.

MATTHEW 9:22

What would it be like to be healed in a moment? Wouldn't it be amazing to meet Jesus, touch Him, and experience His healing? This woman in the Bible experienced God as Healer immediately because of her faith.

When I read this passage, I wish my faith was stronger. I have a hard time believing in what I don't see (Hebrews 1:1). I tend to focus on what seems logical to my human mind, but I want to believe God can move mountains in my life and the lives of others today (Matthew 17:20–21). Some of my favorite Sundays at our church are ones when there is no sermon and people instead volunteer to share their "God stories." Hearing about a scan that showed cancer or disease and it no longer being there after people prayed for healing strengthens my faith and reminds me that God is still supernaturally working miracles today.

Turning to Father God and asking for what we want or need strengthens our faith. Experiencing answered prayers or looking back and seeing His healing makes it more likely we will turn to Him again instead of trying to handle it on our own or giving up and feeling hopeless. I have gone through seasons of life where I and those around me experienced such severe suffering that I become discouraged and begin to wonder if God is still working miracles and answering prayers. When that happens, sometimes I'll open a past journal where I've recorded answers to prayers or call a woman of faith and ask her to share a recent answer to prayer she experienced. Let's continue to ask God to heal our bodies, minds, and hearts and trust Him to do miracles. When answers come, let's record them and share them, reminding others to keep praying and trusting our Father through His Holy Spirit to work in and through us all.

Experiencing Father God's Healing

Father, I confess to You that I lack faith. It's hard to believe what I cannot see. Please grow my faith by pointing out Your healing in my life. Surround me with others whose faith is greater than mine. May their testimonies of Your healing give me hope to believe. Amen.

Growing Stronger

Read Matthew 9 and focus on the passages of healing Jesus performed. Talk to your heavenly Father about the desires you have for healing in your own life and ask Him to perform miracles just as He did back then.

1

The Filler

LYNN

"Come, all you who are thirsty, come to the waters; and you who have no money, come, buy and eat! Come, buy wine and milk without money and without cost."

ISAIAH 55:1

Even though you were afraid, you opened your heart, sharing something personal with someone. Then, in the middle of this vulnerable moment, they picked up their phone and began scrolling. Was the realness too much for them? Did it make them uncomfortable or bored? Was something more important demanding their attention? I would imagine you've experienced this kind of neglect just like I have. It hurts when someone doesn't recognize how important their undivided attention is to you.

When you bare your heart to Father God, you can be confident you have His complete attention. Because He created you, He understands you completely, and He loves you just as you are!

Think of people like pitchers of water. When your heart is empty, broken, rejected, or sad, going to others to be patched up or filled is helpful. As they pour their love, attention, and encouragement into you, you feel better. Over time, if your need for their love, attention, and encouragement is greater than their ability (the "water" they carry), their pitcher can then get depleted. Maybe due to their own struggles, they lack reserves to give to others. Their love, attention, and encouragement may run dry.

Your Father God is not a pitcher that runs out; He's more like a faucet. You can go to Him, and He will turn on the water of His love, understanding, patience, and healing to fill you repeatedly, no matter how needy you are (John 7:38). Every moment of every day, He can fill your heart. He never comes close to being empty!

Your Father gives you an invitation to come to Him in our verse for today, Isaiah 55:1. He is never annoyed or too busy. Quite the opposite; four times in this verse, He says, "Come!"

Experiencing Father God's Healing

Is there an area of your life where you feel like God is worn out from hearing from you or is tired of you? Know that this is simply not possible with your Father! Talk to Him about it again today.

Growing Stronger

Read all of Isaiah 55. Which part of this verse gives you the most hope and why? Share on the lines below.

8

Best Doctor Ever

MICHELLE

Jesus answered them, "It is not the healthy who need a doctor, but the sick."

LUKE 5:31

I hate being sick! I feel like every time I have a cold, stomach problems, or an injury, I miss out on the fun things in life. Also, being in bed puts me behind on the things I need to get done, so when I am well again, I feel overwhelmed trying to catch up. In junior high and high school, I was so sick, I missed an entire week of school and activities. When I returned, I not only needed to do all my current assignments but also the ones I'd missed. Math was superhard; I felt lost in class since I hadn't been there to learn the lessons I needed to understand before I could do the problems we were currently working on. Choir and tennis could be even worse, with my directors and coaches wanting me to quickly learn the music I needed to perform or make up the matches I needed to play. Even though I felt better physically, I often struggled with discouragement. I felt like I just couldn't do it all.

Our Father wants to be our Great Physician whether we are sick physically or mentally. He wants to heal us and help us hold on to hope that we will recover fully. Sometimes He gives us the strength to catch up, sometimes He gives us the courage to ask for extensions, and sometimes He give us permission to leave it unfinished and suffer the consequences. I look back on those moments in school that seemed like life or death and realize now that I not only survived, but those moments also made me better and more compassionate when

I work with kids who are struggling. I was a teacher who gave grace, a counselor who understood, and now a parent who realizes that not everything is as big a deal as it might seem. I help my kids to do what they can and am okay if they have to take a lower grade or move on.

Experiencing Father God's Healing

Father, thank You for caring about me when I'm sick. When I need doctors, send me ones who have wise minds, skilled hands, and compassionate hearts. Give my teachers and parents understanding and remind them that it's hard to be behind and need to catch up. Thanks for offering me understanding, compassion, and healing when I'm sick or have been sick. Be the Healer of my body, mind, soul, and relationships. Amen.

Growing Stronger

If you or a friend are feeling behind and feeling overwhelmed today, pray for healing, grace, and peace. Offer yourself or someone else a word of encouragement that God's got this, and no matter how far behind you or she feels, it's going to be okay. One grading period doesn't determine the rest of your life.

9

Keep Going and Keep Growing

LYNN

For as high as the heavens are above the earth, so great is his love for those who fear him; as far as the east is from the west, so far has he removed our transgressions from us.

PSALM 103:11–12

ave you ever had someone remind you over and over of a mistake you made? A responsibility you failed to fulfill? A flaw that keeps showing up again and again? The person may not intend to crush you, but the hurtful words can cause you to become stuck, feeling helpless to change. Our minds may tell us, *You'll always be this way because you've always been this way.*

Painful words spoken, heart now hurting, and mind then believing can become a vicious cycle unless we stop the spinning with the truth of God's Word. The psalmist wrote in Psalm 103:11–12: "For as high as the heavens are above the earth, so great is his love for those who fear him; as far as the east is from the west, so far has he removed our transgressions from us."

These verses give us so much hope! When we sin, it doesn't mean we're doomed to repeat that behavior over and over. When we ask the Father to forgive us, He does! Each and every time you come to Him, He doesn't say to you, *This is the twenty-fifth time you've come to Me asking for forgiveness and help.* His patience and love flow unlimited toward us as we seek to become more like Him. He says He removes our sins "as far as the east is from the west."

As far as the east is from the west—that is a hard concept for me. Is it for you?

I have an old-school 3D globe sitting on the shelf in my office for a decoration. (You can see an example of a globe by searching "globe earth 3-D video.") If I keep spinning the globe in one direction, it keeps going and going and going. It never suddenly stops and reverses direction. East never becomes west. East and west *never* meet.

God tells us in this passage that His forgiveness is infinite. He doesn't keep score of our sins or remind us of them later on. When we purpose to respect and honor Him with our lives, yet still sin, He forgives us and we can walk confidently as forgiven daughters.

Experiencing Father God's Healing

Being reminded of past failures doesn't help us stop repeating failures. Being close to our Father does. Read today's passage of Psalm 103:11–12 out loud, reminding yourself how God's forgiveness works.

Growing Stronger

Read Psalm 103:6–14. Which characteristics of God encourage you that He is for you? Share your thoughts on the lines below.

10

Faithful When We Struggle

MICHELLE

If we are unfaithful, he remains faithful, for he cannot deny who he is.

2 TIMOTHY 2:13 NLT

In my forties, I was diagnosed with ADHD, but when I became a counselor in my twenties, I knew I struggled with many of the symptoms. I love doing a variety of activities, including learning new things, because they create the neurochemical dopamine in my brain. I have always been able to hyperfocus when I loved what I was doing or when I had procrastinated and was now under a deadline. The adrenaline my body produced when I needed to finish a short assignment or study for a test worked well for me because God gave me a fast brain and an above-average memory. But as the work got harder and longer, like writing papers, I struggled to meet the deadlines or turn in the quality of work that I knew I could do and was expected of me. I needed more structure to be successful.

Today, deadlines for books like the one you're reading have resurrected my large-project struggles. I often feel like I'm not being faithful to my calling or a good steward of the talents God has given me. In moments like these, I've learned to cry out to my Father and ask others for help, encouragement, and even accountability. God is faithful to help us when we struggle. Our Father wants us to experience success. He doesn't lecture us or shame us for our weaknesses. Father God understands our shortcomings because He is our creator.

Experiencing Father God's Healing

If you've fallen behind in your schoolwork or on life tasks like paying bills or cleaning your room, first talk to Father God and tell Him your struggles. Pour it all out in a journal or in prayer like you would if you were talking to a friend or parent. Trust in His faithfulness to help you. His help can encourage you to be brave enough to acknowledge your weaknesses and seek help from others, such as a counselor, tutor, or life coach.

If you, like me, have a diagnosis such as ADHD or anxiety, you might need to access your campus disability services so that you can receive extended time on your assignments. When I've had the courage to talk with my teachers, professors, and now editors and ask for help, they have not only worked with me on catching up but encouraged me to continue persevering.

Growing Stronger

Come up with a plan of action to help you when you fall behind or struggle. Seek out resources that God can use to come alongside you when you fall behind.

11

Out of the Maze

LYNN

*Trust in the L ORD with all your heart and lean
not on your own understanding; in all your ways
submit to him, and he will make your paths
straight.*

PROVERBS 3:5–6

What is your favorite season? Me? I love fall! Give me all of the pumpkin spice lattes, sweatshirts, football, cozy blankets, and hikes in the mountain fog.

There is one thing you can keep, though: corn mazes. Corn mazes and I just don't get along. Even if there is a promise of hot chocolate and warm treats at the end, my experience when I can't find the way out only leads to anxiety. Usually, someone has to come in through the exit to get me out. What is supposed to be fun is frustrating.

Mazes resemble another area of my life where I've ended up frustrated: people-pleasing. Looking to people to fill my needs for acceptance and approval, I've gotten caught in a confusing puzzle, a pattern that makes no sense to me. After trying so hard to make other people happy, usually I end up anxious, exhausted, and hurt . . . and often they are still not happy!

Through my own journey of studying God's Word and working with counselors, I've discovered that the more I understand God's character and His love for me, the less I'm tempted to enter into the maze of people-pleasing. Instead, I can make a choice to rely on the Lord for the acceptance and approval I need, not in how much people like me.

When I focus on pleasing the Lord instead of people, the fear of people rejecting me loosens its grip. I'm not expecting myself to win others' acceptance, nor am I dependent on others' acceptance to be okay with being me. In fact, I can honestly say *now* that I'm at peace knowing some people just won't like me. It's all right because I know how much the Father loves me!

Today's proverb gives us a better pattern for living: trusting in the Lord and choosing not to go the direction that seems right to us, the direction of living to make others happy. God's way brings the peace and healing we need.

Experiencing Father God's Healing

Are there any areas in your life where you're caught in the maze of people-pleasing? How does your desire to be well-liked impact your well-being on a day-to-day basis? Write your thoughts on the lines below.

Growing Stronger

Read Proverbs 3 in your Bible, and underline passages that provide principles for leading a healthy life.

12

When You Feel Like No One Cares

MICHELLE

> *"But I will restore you to health and heal your wounds," declares the LORD, "because you are called an outcast, Zion for whom no one cares."*

JEREMIAH 30:17

Ever been rejected by a friend group, or felt like no one cares about you or what you are going through? I've never met a person who hasn't at some point in their life. When I feel this way, I remember that our Father's own Son knows what it's like to be an outcast. While on earth, He was rejected by the religious leaders who you would think would have welcomed Him. One of the men who was closest to Jesus, His disciple Judas, sold Him out for silver (Matthew 26:15). Peter, who was in Jesus's inner circle, denied he knew Jesus three times (Matthew 26:69–75). When Jesus knew He was facing death, He asked His disciples to pray, and they fell asleep (Matthew 26:37–45).

Father God wants to restore us to health and heal our wounds. You may want to give up on people or feel tempted to isolate yourself and hide in your room. Although you may need some time to withdraw and heal, don't wait too long to allow yourself to be vulnerable and ask for help from others.

Experiencing Father God's Healing

Knowing someone is praying for you can remind you of God's faithfulness when you feel like an outcast. Your prayer request can be unspoken. Call a local church and ask to be put on their prayer chain or fill out a form online. (My local church, Resonate Life, has a place at www.resonatelive.tv/prayer.) You can also put your request in the comments of a daily posted devotional like the one Lynn writes for Proverbs 31 Ministries. Many Christian radio stations also have prayer request lines. I would love to pray for you. Feel free to comment on my social media when I ask for prayer requests or fill out the contact form on my website. I may not be able to send a response, but I will pray.

Growing Stronger

When I need God's healing, I often do an exercise I learned in college from Louie Giglio. I see it as the ABCs of God. Think of a word that begins with each letter of the alphabet that also describes Father God. I'll get you started. *A*: He is able. *B*: His works are beautiful. *C*: He is capable. *D*: He is a God of dreams.

13

You, Always

LYNN

Trust God, my friends, and always tell him each of your concerns. God is our place of safety.

PSALM 62:8 CEV

You always do that! You always have!" The hurtful words hurled at me cut straight to my heart. I had really been trying to change and I knew I was growing. But one day, the old behavior came back and someone pointed a finger, reminding me of my past.

Do you have an area you're trying to change and someone feels it's not happening fast enough? You are growing, even if it's slow. You are becoming more responsible, unselfish, on time, or careful with your words. Yet this change is being dismissed, and instead you continue to hear the words, "You always _____ (fill in the blank with your own weakness, shortcomings, or sins)."

When others remind us of our failures, they can feel unsafe. We can feel as though they're not on our side, seeing the growth that *is* happening. Their words hurt.

There is one "always" that gives me comfort when I have been hurt by another's words. Psalm 62:8 tells us: "Trust God, my friends, and always tell him each of your concerns. God is our place of safety" (CEV). We can trust God to *always* be a safe place for us. We can trust Him with our deepest secrets and innermost thoughts. He is our safe place. He will not remind us, ever, of our past sins, shortcomings, or failures because of His promise that "as far as the east is from the west, so far has he removed our transgressions from us" (Psalm 103:12).

Experiencing Father God's Healing

When others hurl hurtful words at you, unforgiveness can easily settle in your heart. Read Psalm 62:8, thanking God that He's always your safe place. Ask Him to empower you to forgive the one who has hurt you, as Colossians 3:13 tells us, "Bear with each other and forgive one another if any of you has a grievance against someone. Forgive as the Lord forgave you."

Growing Stronger

Using a Bible app or website such as Biblehub.com or Biblegateway.com, look up Psalm 62 in the Contemporary English Version (CEV). This verse is full of comforting words. Which one is most meaningful to you today? Share your thoughts in the space below.

14

Healing from Sinful Habits

MICHELLE

I said, "Have mercy on me, LORD; heal me, for I have sinned against you."

PSALM 41:4

Sometimes I keep eating when I've had enough even though I know I need to stop."

"I keep avoiding things I need to get done, just lying around and watching TV instead."

"I want to embrace a biblical worldview, but I can't seem to resist scrolling and comparing myself to others to the point I become discouraged."

Many of the problems people seek Christian counseling for are not only clinical diagnoses but also character issues. Character issues are like a plant. They don't just occur overnight but grow out of repeating poor choices. We start with a little lie that leads to a bigger cover-up. We drink one drink at a party, accidentally get tipsy, like the feeling of losing control, and then seek that experience as a way of escaping life stresses. Late nights lead to sleeping in on mornings when we need to be in class or be productive, and then we continue the pattern to escape the guilt we feel.

Our Father desires to heal us from our sins and empower us to break bad habits. Our first step in healing is to face our sin, confess it to God, and thank Him for His forgiveness. When we turn to God with our sins, He lovingly responds. You won't hear, "Well, it's about time." Those are the words of the Enemy and misguided humans. Instead, you will be greeted with, *I'm so glad you came to Me. You are loved. I want to help you.* We need God's help not just daily but moment by moment in order to choose His ways instead of our own.

Experiencing Father God's Healing

Confession is good for the soul. Today, speak or write out every sin you are struggling with that comes to mind, knowing your sins were forgiven over two thousand years ago on the cross. After you've purged yourself of the weight of sin, spend a moment receiving God's forgiveness and healing. I love attending retreats where we nail these sins—represented in writings—to a wooden cross, write them on tiles and break them, or burn them in a fire.

Growing Stronger

Confession is good for the soul but repentance is good for your life. Repentance involves the hard process of changing your bad habits. The beginning stages of healing include revealing what we've been hiding and facing the consequences we've been avoiding. Healing often requires letting go of prideful independence and receiving help from a support group, sponsor, or professional. Today, choose a sin you confessed and take a step toward true repentance. When you choose to break free of the bondage in your life by repenting of your sins and seeking help, you will experience Father God's freedom.

15

You Get Me

LYNN

*Praise be to the God and Father of our Lord Jesus
Christ, the Father of compassion and the God of
all comfort, who comforts us in all our troubles, so
that we can comfort those in any trouble with the
comfort we ourselves receive from God. For just as
we share abundantly in the sufferings of Christ, so
also our comfort abounds through Christ.*

2 CORINTHIANS 1:3–5

*Y*ou just don't understand!" When my daughter was growing up, I
would often hear these words from her. It tore me up that she felt
this way, and yet to some degree she was right. It wasn't possible for me
to see into her heart and mind, to fully know the pain she was feeling
and give her perfect compassion.

Have you ever experienced true compassion? Someone who deeply
understands the difficulty you are experiencing? Paul described God as
"the Father of compassion and the God of all comfort." The word **compassion** in the original Greek means a "deep feeling about someone's
difficulty or misfortune."*

You may or may not have a person on earth who gives you this deep
level of compassion and comfort. (I hope you do.) But no matter what,
God's Word tells us you can find soothing relief in the God who does in

---

* *HELPS Word-studies*, 2 Cor. 1:3 "οἰκτιρμῶν (oiktirmōn)," word for "Father of mercies,"
accessed March 24, 2024, https://biblehub.com/greek/3628.htm.

fact completely get you! He *created* you, so not only does He understand you, He can comfort you and lessen your sadness in a way that only the One who made you can.

While it's normal for us to long to be completely known inside and out, with humans that's just not possible. Humans don't have the ability to know a person this clearly. We are limited in our ability to understand one another. Not so with our Father! Because the Holy Spirit lives in those of us who are His, He can soothe our hearts and give us joy again.

Experiencing Father God's Healing

Psalm 139:2 tells us, "You know when I sit and when I rise; you perceive my thoughts from afar." Is there a part of you that you feel no one understands? Write about it in the space below. Now, shut your eyes for a moment and thank Father God that He understands! He recognizes everything about you because He created you uniquely with His purposes in mind.

Growing Stronger

Today and in the days ahead, repeat Psalm 139:2 three times a day as a way of giving thanks to God: "You know when I sit and when I rise; you perceive my thoughts from afar."

16

The Practice of Abundant Peace

MICHELLE

"Nevertheless, I will bring health and healing to it; I will heal my people and will let them enjoy abundant peace and security."

JEREMIAH 33:6

When you think of abundant peace and security, what comes to your mind? **Abundant** to me would mean not only enough but extra. Could you use some extra peace? What would that look like in your life?

I often encourage clients having panic attacks, who are struggling with stress, worry, and anxiety, to store up extra calm so that when the panic comes, their bodies will start at a calmer point. This will help them to be able to reclaim calm, because they have practiced skills like meditating on God's Word, breath prayers of breathing in God's peace and breathing out their worries, and releasing tension in their bodies through spiritual stretching. I use the term **spiritual stretching** to mean practicing deep breathing while stretching to praise music or meditating on Scripture. The skill of calming your heart, mind, and body demands dedicated time no different than you would spend preparing for a race. If you were to prepare for a race, you'd set aside time to run, buy special equipment, and maybe join a running group or get a coach. You may need some of these same tools in order to experience the abundant peace your heavenly Father is offering you. When you have reserves stored up, you will discover a security that you've never known before because instead of running on empty, your peace tank will be full.

Experiencing Father God's Healing

Right now, take a moment to breathe and practice cultivating peace in your mind and body. Start with deep breaths. If you have trouble sitting still, you can move your arms up and down with your breaths or lie down with your knees up and turn your hips while moving both your legs from side to side. This can create an emotional or somatic release. Feel your heavenly Father's love shine upon you, releasing any tension in your muscles. Allow His peace to relax your shoulders, expand your heart, and calm your stomach.

Growing Stronger

Choose a time daily or once a week to practice the peace of God in your life so that you can store up some extra for stressful times. Enter this time in your calendar. You might meditate on Isaiah 26:3: "You will keep in perfect peace those whose minds are steadfast, because they trust in you."

17

More Than Dust

LYNN

As a father has compassion on his children, so
the LORD has compassion on those who fear him;
for he knows how we are formed, he remembers
that we are dust.

PSALM 103:13–14

Once again in my teen years, I didn't do what I said I would do and someone reminded me how I had failed. It didn't take long before I began to think of myself as a failure, as a person who never followed through. I was critical of myself whenever I didn't do something perfectly. Growing more and more uptight and rigid, I had no sense of what "grace" or "mercy" meant.

Today, I have more compassion for my younger self. I realize children are easily distracted. I was learning what it meant to be responsible and follow through on what I said I would do. My mistakes didn't mean being irresponsible would always define me. Now I know: God has compassion on me when I mess up and I can have compassion on myself too.

Psalm 103:13–14 says, "As a father has compassion on his children, so the LORD has compassion on those who fear him; for he knows how we are formed, he remembers that we are dust." The psalmist is assuming we have human fathers who are loving like our heavenly Father. Father God gets how we are made because He is the One who made us! Genesis 2:7 tells us, "Then the LORD God formed a man from the dust of the ground and breathed into his nostrils the breath of life, and the man became a living being." The Father understands us and how we work.

Because He made us, He understands that we are humans who make mistakes. He has grace and is patient with us, even when we mess up. Since He has grace and patience with me, I can have grace and patience with me too!

Experiencing Father God's Healing

In what area of your life do you need to give yourself more compassion? Write about this in the space below. Ask the Father to help you to understand His unending compassion and help you to have compassion on yourself as well.

_____

_____

_____

_____

_____

_____

_____

_____

_____

Growing Stronger

Read all of Psalm 103 in a translation or paraphrase that is different from what you usually read, perhaps the Amplified Bible, *The Message*, or The Voice. (You can find these versions on Biblegateway.com.) Which characteristic of God do you feel you understand the least and would benefit from learning more about?

18

Healing Through Praise

MICHELLE

*Heal me, LORD, and I will be healed; save
me and I will be saved, for you are the
one I praise.*

JEREMIAH 17:14

*O*ften counseling and helping people can be very problem-centered instead of solution-focused. We get trapped in a looping mindset, focusing on what's wrong and looking back to discover where it came from instead of creating a plan of change so we do something different in the future. When I was younger, I tended to look only at what was wrong with me. I've also been around Christians who tend to focus solely on sin. Being solution-focused is different. Like positive psychology, we direct people to look at their strengths and what has worked before in their healing journey. We help them change their focus to the outcome instead of trying to figure out the why and the how. This method allows healing to occur faster.

When our problems seem too big, reminding ourselves that Father God is bigger than our worries gives us hope. When we praise Him, we are reminded of all His amazing characteristics. Physically moving and using our vocal cords also helps our bodies release built-up stress and tension that comes from hours of sitting, learning, and doing homework. Praise brings healing as it reminds us of God's truth and defeats the lies the Enemy tempts us to believe about ourselves and our futures.

Experiencing Father God's Healing

Find or make a praise and worship playlist and then make a joyful, loud noise. Move your body if possible so that your body can experience healing as well as your mind and heart. As you sing about God's power and goodness, envision Him entering those hard places in your life. See the face of the person you are struggling with, that class you dread attending, or feel that feeling you feel when you want to run away. Then continue to praise Him, letting His presence overshadow all of the distractions in your life.

Growing Stronger

Dedicate times for praise in your life. If you like quiet, play instrumental hymns or worship. Attend a praise and worship service at a church other than your own. Sing during your weekly drive or when you are getting ready for the day or in the shower. Turn off Instagram or your guilty-pleasure podcast and open up your favorite music app and blast some praise and worship or take a praise walk where you listen and hum to worship music. Humming is another great way to release tension in your body.

19

You Keep Them All

LYNN

*Record my misery; list my tears on your scroll—
are they not in your record?*

PSALM 56:8

How do you feel about tears? Are they good? Are they bad? Do you see them as something to hold back or do you think it's best to let them flow?

For many of us, the way we view tears has to do with the way we've been brought up. I really like Psalm 56:8 because it reveals God's perspective on our tears: they're precious to Him.

God's Word contains passages describing how God not only cares when we grieve, but that He also grieves. John 11:1–44 tells the story of Jesus's heart aching when His dear friend Lazarus died.

In Psalm 56:8, God is said to collect all our tears in a bottle. The tear bottle is a tradition that is over three thousand years old. In biblical times, mourners would collect their tears in small bottles and then bury the bottles with their loved ones, showing their deep love for them.* The psalmist used this tradition as a way to explain just how much our Father cares about our sorrows and what causes us pain. He's collecting our tears; He is recording them in a book, showing He values them. In fact, God designed our ability to cry in a way that is tied to healing. Crying can bring comfort as our tears release feel-good chemicals

HEALER

---

* http://www.lachrymatory.com/, accessed June 4, 2024.

called endorphins in our brains, reducing the pain we're feeling in both our bodies and our hearts.[†]

Experiencing Father God's Healing

How does it make you feel knowing the Father collects your tears? Describe this in the space below.

_____

_____

_____

_____

_____

_____

_____

_____

_____

_____

_____

_____

_____

_____

Growing Stronger

Read John 11:1–44. How does Jesus respond to sorrow in verse 33? Why do you think He responded this way when He knew that soon He would raise Lazarus from the dead?

20

Healing Through You

MICHELLE

"Heal the sick, raise the dead, cleanse those who have leprosy, drive out demons. Freely you have received; freely give."

MATTHEW 10:8

Do you have the spiritual gift of healing? Since I felt called to ministry at sixteen, I have pursued being equipped by God to be a vessel of healing for others. I love comforting the brokenhearted, empowering clients to retrain their brains and renew their minds, and encouraging them to embrace freedom in Christ as they navigate a tough world.

How has Father God healed you? I've known people whose prayers for physical healing were answered by God through cancerous tumors shrinking without medical intervention. Others, like myself, have found healing from pain through a doctor, surgery, and physical therapy. During revivals and worship services, I've heard testimonies of people delivered from their desire to drink or overeat. Clients in my office have claimed God's deliverance from a spirit of fear that had crippled them for years. Our Father longs for us to seek His healing presence and, with whatever faith we have, ask for emotional, mental, spiritual, and relational healing.

Recently, I received God's healing touch from a neighbor. While we were out walking our dogs, she asked how I was. As I responded with "Okay," tears I couldn't stop escaped from my eyes. I shared that I was struggling with sadness as it was the one-year anniversary of my dad's death. My doorbell rang not even thirty minutes later. My neighbor held in her hands a few slices of homemade sweet bread filled with chocolate. Her kindness brought healing to my heart. I call these moments "God glimmers." Our Father shows His love to us through the kindness of others, reminding us He sees us and cares when our days are hard.

How could you share a God glimmer of healing with others? Could you pray faithfully (regularly and often) for someone, seeking updates so they know they haven't been forgotten? This week a six-year-old girl in our community has been in the children's ICU struggling to breathe. We've gathered together in prayer meetings, written our prayers in a prayer journal, set up a prayer wall, and shared new prayer requests as she's progressed. Joined together, we've witnessed the Father at work.

But sometimes, even though we pray really hard, God doesn't always bring healing on earth. Loss and grief are devastating realities of a broken world. In those moments, I long for heaven, where there will be no more death and mourning (Revelation 21:1–4).

Experiencing Father God's Healing

Find someone in your life who needs healing. Commit to pray for them often and ask for updates. You might voice record or write out a prayer for them and send it. Hearing someone else pray for us can encourage us and strengthen our faith when we feel weak.

Growing Stronger

Read Mark 5:24–34. Ask your Father for a strong faith that will inspire you to reach out to Him for healing.

Peace

MEDITATION MATTERS

"I have told you these things, so that in me you may have peace. In this world you will have trouble. But take heart! I have overcome the world."

JOHN 16:33

You will keep in perfect peace those whose minds are steadfast, because they trust in you.

ISAIAH 26:3

Therefore my heart is glad and my tongue rejoices; my body also will rest secure.

PSALM 16:9

1

Peace Is Who You Are

LYNN

So Gideon built an altar to the LORD there and called it The LORD Is Peace. To this day it stands in Ophrah of the Abiezrites.

JUDGES 6:24

Sometimes it feels like everything is going wrong! Plans fall apart. Friends have fights. Things break. You begin to wonder, *What is going on?*

In Judges 6, God's people also wrestled with a season of struggle. The Israelites had enemies called the Midianites. These enemies had stolen their food and their land. Things had gotten so bad that the people had moved out of their cities and were hiding in mountains and caves! God saw what was happening and chose someone to help. His name was Gideon. In Judges 6:11, the angel of the Lord came to visit Gideon.

When the angel said, "The LORD is with you, mighty warrior" (v. 12), Gideon disagreed. Gideon asked the Lord to explain. If the Lord was with them and Gideon was a mighty warrior, he wondered, why were they having so many troubles with their enemies? God reassured Gideon by telling him, "Go in the strength you have and save Israel out of Midian's hand. Am I not sending you?" (v. 14).

Gideon came back again with a rebuttal, pointing out his personal weaknesses. The Lord also came back with His own rebuttal. "I will be with you," He reassured Gideon (v. 16). God's last words to Gideon were,

"Peace! Do not be afraid" (v. 23). After this final statement, Gideon built an altar to the Lord and called it "The LORD is Peace" (v. 24).

This story is important for us to know because Father God not only gives us peace, peace is *who* He is. In fact, one of His names is Yahweh Shalom: The Lord is Peace. His peace is more than just a feeling we experience. It also isn't something He just gives. Peace is His character.

Gideon went on to face unsurmountable obstacles and troubles, yet Peace Himself was with him. And in the end, Gideon and his men completely defeated their enemy.

Experiencing Father God's Peace

We are told that our enemy is Satan: "The thief comes only to steal and kill and destroy" (John 10:10). Our fight is not against people but against dark, spiritual forces (Ephesians 6:12). Some of our unseen enemies look like self-doubt, guilt, confusion, apathy, unforgiveness, and so on. Enemies that prevent us from living calmly. We can find rest and peace knowing Yahweh Shalom, the Lord is Peace, is always with us. Where do you need to experience Father God's peace in your life today? Share in the space below.

Growing Stronger

Read Gideon's entire thrilling story in Judges 6. What might you and Gideon have in common?

2

Peace with God

MICHELLE

> *Therefore, since we have been justified through faith, we have peace with God through our Lord Jesus Christ.*

ROMANS 5:1

Guilt prevents us from being at peace with God. When I was a youth minister, guilt struggles seemed to constantly haunt my female students. Junior high girls often make lots of promises to themselves regarding sex and sexuality, drinking and using drugs, not watching porn, self-harm, and even how they will treat others. Back then we even had these conferences called "True Love Waits." While I believe waiting until marriage to have sex is definitely best, I talk with many older high school and college women who no longer have that choice as their reality. They beat themselves up, and often the guilt and shame they feel drives them toward an "I don't care" attitude that leads to an increase in unhealthy sexual activities as they attempt to disconnect from the guilt.

All of us sin, and what makes us pure is not our choices but Jesus's living sacrifice on the cross for each one of us. Choosing Jesus as Lord and Savior is the only way to fully experience peace with God. With that choice comes forgiveness for the sins we have done and the sins we will do in the future.

Our Father's forgiveness releases us from the patterns of our past and empowers us to walk in freedom to make different future choices. Will you trust the work of Jesus on the cross to bring you peace for whatever you've felt couldn't be forgiven today?

Experiencing Father God's Peace

Father, I need to experience Your forgiveness today so that I won't continue to sin against You tomorrow. May the freedom You offer release me from the chains that keep me bound to the person in the past I no longer am. Help me to walk as a new creation in Christ today (2 Corinthians 5:17). Amen.

Growing Stronger

Today, commit to no longer dwell on your past mistakes that you cannot change. Remind yourself of the following each time your mind tries to get you to look back: There is no shame for Christ followers (Romans 8:1). You are free!

3

Even in the Dark

LYNN

"I have told you these things, so that in me you may have peace. In this world you will have trouble. But take heart! I have overcome the world."

JOHN 16:33

Loneliness surged over me in the darkness of my bedroom. This move from a Christian school to a public school was way harder than I'd anticipated. Somehow, I thought I would slip right back into the friend group I had when I went to public school with the neighborhood kids. I had forgotten one huge element: we had all changed. I wasn't the same kid; nor were they.

Listening to sad music in my dark bedroom only fed the rejection ruminating in my heart. *Why am I alone on a Friday night again?* As I contemplated the answer, I considered the path my life had taken over the past few months. Some decisions had absolutely been mine; others, not so much.

Yet even in that difficult moment, I sensed Father God providing the comfort I needed that *He* was with me. Though it was difficult, I hadn't, in fact, made the wrong move. Sometimes following His way, though it is the *best* way, is also the hard way. He said it would be so. "I have told you these things, so that in me you may have peace. In this world you will have trouble. But take heart! I have overcome the world" (John 16:33).

Peace. Peace is what Father God provided in that hard place. He didn't fix my loneliness struggles or make my troubles go away. I didn't suddenly have an amazing friend group or someone who would call me each night and say how much they liked me. What I could experience in Him was *His* peaceful presence with me.

God's peace can envelop you in the dark night of your room as well as the bright lights of the school halls. No matter where you are, His peace can be with you because He is with you and for you.

Experiencing Father God's Peace

Where do you struggle most to experience your Father's peace? When you get up to bat? When you hear your parents arguing? As you scroll through your social media? Right now, focus fully and begin to recite to yourself the words of Jesus: *"I have overcome the world."* Jesus has overcome the world. No matter what we are experiencing, His power and peace that is available to us is greater than anything.

Growing Stronger

Read 1 John 4:4. How can this verse influence the struggle you just thought about above? Share in the space below.

4

Because We Trust Him

MICHELLE

You will keep in perfect peace those whose minds are steadfast, because they trust in you.

ISAIAH 26:3

I know I'm supposed to trust God, but why is it so hard?" I often hear this question as I sit across from Christians young and old.

We live in a broken world. We can do good things that we believe should lead to certain results, but they don't. Sometimes the girl making wrong decisions gets the guy who seems perfect for you. Sometimes you study for a test and still get a bad grade. People trust God and still get sick, hurt, and have bad things happen to them.

God's promised peace can happen on the inside of us no matter what is occurring in our lives today. When we trust the Father with our lives, it doesn't mean that everything will work out the way we think it should, but it does mean that when we focus on Him, what's going on around us seems less important than being in His presence. Moving our mind's focus away from life circumstances and onto a powerful, loving heavenly Father allows the Holy Spirit to fill us with the peace of God.

Experiencing Father God's Peace

Isaiah 26:3 promises peace to those whose minds are steadfast. **Steadfast** can mean loyal. Loyalty to God would mean putting Him above anyone else in our lives. A steadfast mind is one that is trained on God more than anything else. Daily, we are tempted by distractions that take our minds off God. Today, take some time to focus on Him.

Psalm 27:4 describes this kind of focus as gazing on the beauty of the Lord. You can do this no matter where you are. Breathe deeply and bring to mind a Scripture, worship song, or even a moment in your life when you strongly sensed God's presence. Choosing small moments throughout your day to gaze upon your Father God will train your brain to sense God's presence and His peace no matter where you are.

Growing Stronger

Read Matthew 8:23–27. Are there storms in your life that are making you feel afraid? Talk to your heavenly Father about what's going on and your fears. Ask Him to give you peace, whether that means He calms the storms in your life or He calms you on the inside.

5

You Are Good

LYNN

You are good, and what you do is good; teach me your decrees.

PSALM 119:68

*H*ave you ever walked into a room knowing something's wrong, but you can't put your finger on it? You caught people sharing looks with one another. *What was said before I walked in?* you wonder. Something is going on. People are smiling, acting nice, and trying to be "normal," but normal is not what's happening.

When that happened to me recently, I found out later that there had been a fight. Someone had been talking about me. Though they were acting as if things between us were good, they weren't being good toward me.

Psalm 119:68 teaches us that Father God is good. Always. It is who He is. He never betrays us. When I am in our Father's presence, I can experience His peace. I trust that what He has for me is good and comes from love because He is love.

With our Father, there is no such thing as manipulation or false motives. Good, which Father God is, does not look out for itself to the detriment of the other person. God never pretends with us.

When God created us, He gave us free will, meaning He has no hidden motives or plans to manipulate us with false guilt, or intentions to force us into obedience by giving us no other choice. Manipulation to get a person to act a certain way does not come from love. It is essential for us to understand this because sometimes the path of following God will be hard. We'll be faced with difficult choices concerning what we will do, who we choose to spend time with, and the way we will go. Keeping our focus on our Father and His pure, untainted love will help us continue following Him.

Knowing Father God is good empowers us to relax and be at peace in His love. With His power, we can choose to pay attention to and focus on His peace within us, not ruminate on anxious or fearful thoughts, because the One who is our Father works all things for our good (Romans 8:28). We can trust Him.

Experiencing Father God's Peace

Father, I am so grateful You are good and You do good. I will find peace today in this truth. In Jesus's name, amen.

Growing Stronger

Look up Isaiah 26:3. What is the action we take in order to experience His perfect peace? Choose a method to keep this verse on your mind today: a note on your phone, a text you send yourself, or a note in your pocket you can pull out.

6

God's Peace Is Different

MICHELLE

"Peace I leave with you; my peace I give you. I do not give to you as the world gives. Do not let your hearts be troubled and do not be afraid."

JOHN 14:27

*A*s our culture focuses on mental health, everywhere you look you can discover a new method for finding peace. I've never in my lifetime seen as many options as we have today. Our counseling center has resources like workbooks, phone apps, and videos to help you cultivate more peace in your brain and body. Additional interventions might include a decluttering, using headphones to block out noise, and lighting candles to create calm for your senses. I love escaping alone to a prayer cabin for a day or two.

Utilizing techniques like these can help for a moment . . . but they rarely last. God is offering us a different kind of peace. Our Father's peace manifests as fruit of the Spirit (Galatians 5:22–23). God's peace can only come to us when we are attached to Him like a vine on a branch (John 15:5). When we remain connected to Him, He changes our perspective from the inside out by flowing in and through us. We experience Father God's peace when we align our thoughts with His thoughts and see the world through His filter. I like to call this the "Father filter." The Father filter makes things of this world seem less meaningful. The Father filter reminds us that this present moment isn't all there is to life. The Father filter gives us hope in a life beyond this one where there will not be pain, wars, rejection, or failure.

Experiencing Father God's Peace

Father, help me use Your filter as I go through my day. Help me experience peace that's not based on what is happening now but is instead rooted in my knowledge that I have a life with You beyond this one. Help me to plug into Your peace and Your perspective. May I be an extension cord of Your love to others. Amen.

Growing Stronger

Read John 15:4–11. Take a moment to focus on the word **abide** (or **remain**, depending on the version you read). What would it look like to abide in Him as you get ready for the day, drive to work or school, spend time with friends, do your work, eat your meals, get ready for bed, and wait to fall asleep?

1

The Source of the Hurting

LYNN

Therefore my heart is glad and my tongue rejoices; my body also will rest secure.

PSALM 16:9

For the second day in a row, my stomach hurts. I've thought back over what I've eaten. I can't remember eating anything that would give me a stomachache. Yet the twisting and turning won't stop.

When I tell my friend about the pain I'm feeling, wondering what's wrong with me, he asks me a question I hadn't considered: "Are you nervous about tomorrow?"

Are you nervous about tomorrow? That is a very good question. Tomorrow, I am spending the day with someone who has hurt my feelings in the past. While they've asked for my forgiveness and I have given it, I wonder if my body is responding in fear to the reality of interacting with them. Only time will reveal if this person has changed and will be safe for me.

As I lie on my bed, I think of this verse in Psalm 16: "Therefore my heart is glad and my tongue rejoices; my body also will rest secure" (v. 9). That's led me to meditate on this verse, saying these words over and over again to myself: *My body also will rest secure.* While I have been praying about this day for quite some time, I recognize that my prayers have been wrapped in anxiety, uncertain about how this interaction will go; I want to protect my heart while trusting God.

It's important for us to realize that sometimes what our bodies experience is an indicator of what is happening inside our hearts. While I've been praying in my mind for tomorrow to go well, my spirit has been wrestling with worry. I need to take a moment now and recognize this lack of peace, reminding myself that God is with me. When I praise Him for being with me and for me, my heart can find the peace and security I need as I move toward Him. This doesn't mean that my anxious feelings will suddenly disappear. It does mean that I can set my mind to trust God and believe that my body will, in time, catch up with the truth that He can be trusted.

Experiencing Father God's Peace

When you have a headache or stomachache, take a moment to think about what is going on in your life. Do you have something stressful taking place where you need your Father to help you and bring His peace? Pray, asking Father God to help you give this situation to Him. You might use a heating pad, warm throw, or weighted blanket to help your body relax. Try lying down and breathing deep breaths. As you breathe in, say to yourself Psalm 16:9: *My heart is glad and my tongue rejoices.* And as you breathe out, say, *My body also will rest secure.*

Growing Stronger

Memorize Psalm 16:9 so that it is ready, at the tip of your memory, when anxiousness is causing you to have unpleasant feelings in your body.

8

Peacemaker vs. Peacekeeper

MICHELLE

And those who are peacemakers will plant seeds
of peace and reap a harvest of righteousness.

JAMES 3:18 NLT

I grew up in a family with lots of conflict. My dad punished us with angry words and a belt instead of practicing peaceful discipline. As I got older, I learned to avoid him and his punishment. My mom helped. She counseled me to be a peacekeeper so I wouldn't be a target. I did this by not asking for what I wanted, not displaying my true feelings, and agreeing to what seemed impossible and then trying to figure it out. He wanted chores done cheerfully and our home to be neat even though we were young, busy outside the home, and—for most of us—bent toward being messy. Grades were important, and being good at something was rewarded with positive attention.

When I was in college, I learned about being a peacemaker—someone who works to create harmony between people—but the idea was hard to put into action. Growing up, I'd kept the peace to avoid conflict. This trauma coping skill, which counselors now identify as "fawning," carried into my relationships with boys and later men. I tried to be who they wanted me to be so they would like me. For a loud, strong woman like myself, that meant pretending to be softer and at times even less smart and spiritual than I really was so they would be less intimidated by me. This kept the peace, but wasn't being a peacemaker.

When I became a peacemaker, I could be myself whether someone chose me or not. I spoke the truth in love, owning how I was created and following my calling to teach even though my church told us that women shouldn't. Being a peacemaker also meant learning to relax and listen to others without feeling a need to defend myself. I learned that conflict didn't have to be combative. I could be friends with and love someone even though we agreed to disagree on things, because we reached a peaceful understanding.

Experiencing Father God's Peace

Father, I confess to You that I often avoid conflict in order to keep the peace. Help me learn to seek You, trust You, and speak truth in love. I know You created me the way I was made for a purpose, but that doesn't mean everyone will like me. Help me realize that if they don't like me, I don't need to be someone I'm not. May I remember that I'm always loved in Your eyes and may that give me the courage to be a peacemaker in Your world.

Growing Stronger

This week, when someone says something critical to you or misunderstands you, seek Father God's strength for the courage to speak up. Share how you felt when you heard their words. Hold on to your truth about who you are, what you believe, and what you were created to do.

9

Slow to Anger

LYNN

The LORD is compassionate and gracious, slow to anger, abounding in love.

PSALM 103:8

As a teenager, there were certain adults I felt I had to be perfect around or they would get irritated. It seemed to take very little to set them off. Somewhere along the way, I began to believe God was the same way as these adults. I thought when I messed up, God would also get angry with me, as if He had a short temper. It wasn't until later in my life that I learned He was just the opposite.

Psalm 103:8 teaches us that our Father "is compassionate and gracious, slow to anger, abounding in love." Father God doesn't look at how I've messed up repeatedly and get angry with me. Father God is not hard to please or easily angered. Love is patient (1 Corinthians 13:4) and God is love (1 John 4:7). His love keeps flowing to me, even when I fail and make a mistake or sin. And He is quick to forgive when I ask.

Today, when people get mad at me, I have to remind myself God is not mad at me too. I am learning, though, that while others see my actions and may assume the worst about me, my Father sees me and understands my heart even more than my actions. When we understand this truth, peace can fill our hearts because our Father's love covers all of our shortcomings.

Experiencing Father God's Peace

Say this prayer to your Father: Father, while others see my actions and assume the worst, You see my heart and understand my actions. Align both my heart and my actions with Your truth, Lord. Amen.

Growing Stronger

Do an internet search using this phrase: "Bible verses that show God is slow to anger." Read a few of the verses given, reassuring your heart of this truth, and write down your favorite here.

10

Gratitude Leads to Peace

MICHELLE

Do not be anxious about anything, but in every situation, by prayer and petition, with thanksgiving, present your requests to God. And the peace of God, which transcends all understanding, will guard your hearts and your minds in Christ Jesus.

PHILIPPIANS 4:6-7

What do you think about that increases your anxiety? For me and my clients, I've found it happens when we worry we don't have enough. Enough time to get things done. Enough money to pay for gas, food, and bills. Enough love and attention from those who are supposed to be there for us. When we focus on what we don't have, it's easy to become overwhelmed with wants or needs. Philippians 4:6–7 beckons us to pray for what we need and want and then shift our focus to what we do have.

Intentionally practicing gratitude to God decreases depression and is shown to increase happiness.[*] We can be grateful that we have 1,440 minutes in a day and 168 hours in a week. If we have our basic needs met—enough food to eat, a place to live, and clothes to wear—we can

---

[*] Yu Komase et al., "Effects of Gratitude Intervention on Mental Health and Well-being Among Workers: A Systematic Review," *Journal of Occupational Health*, 63, no. 1 (January): e12290, https://www.ncbi.nlm.nih.gov/pmc/articles/PMC8582291/.

rejoice in God's provision. If we can name a few people who love us, we can be grateful for them. Lately, I've been grateful for my health and ability to move without pain. Some days I'm grateful for excellent weather or having a fun activity planned in the near future.

I hope my list gets you thinking and helps you create a mindset shift if you've been tempted, like I am, to focus more on things that are stressing me out or worries about future problems that might not even come to be.

Experiencing Father God's Peace

Father, it's so easy to look around at what others have and get worked up about what I don't. The Enemy loves to make me feel unloved and needy. Help me to remember You are the source of all I need. May I remember to count my blessings and ask You for what I want. Amen.

Growing Stronger

Start a practice of gratitude today by observing three things you are grateful for that have occurred in the last twenty-four hours. Maybe you survived a test, had a friend to walk with, or received an answer to prayer. Pray or write out in short sentences the following: Father, I thank You for time with _____. Thank You for helping me finish _____. I'm so grateful for _____.

11

My Refuge

LYNN

The LORD is a refuge for the oppressed, a stronghold in times of trouble. Those who know your name trust in you for you, O LORD, have not forsaken those who seek you.

PSALM 9:9-10

When I was growing up, somehow, I learned these two false beliefs:

1. If I followed God and did life according to what I thought the Bible said, I wouldn't have any troubles.
2. Troubles only happened to those who followed their own way in life, not God's.

I guess admitting to believing these two false beliefs meant I didn't know God's Word well enough, or if I did, I didn't really understand what it said. In Psalm 9:9, David, a man who loved God and followed God, wrote: "The LORD is a refuge for the oppressed, a stronghold in times of trouble." David knew something I didn't. Sometimes bad things happen to good people.

The word **oppressed** in this verse could also be translated as **crushed.*** David wrote these words because he knew what it was to be

---

* *Strong's Concordance*, s.v. "dak (*adj.*)," accessed March 24, 2024, https://biblehub.com /hebrew/1790.htm.

crushed *and* he experienced God being his peace, safe place, and shelter from life's storms.

When I was growing up, I knew when I didn't get invited to parties and hangouts, it was usually because I followed Jesus. I tried to avoid doing what my conscience told me was wrong. While I knew God's way was the best in the long run, these rejections still left me feeling lonely and left out. Sometimes I forgot when I was in those tough times that the Lord was my refuge, comfort, and peace for my aching heart.

Choosing to seek Father God, trusting He will lead us to His peace even in the middle of our troubles, doesn't make our problems disappear. But Father God can give us the peace we need, the comfort our aching hearts crave, as we trust Him.

Experiencing Father God's Peace

Think of a place you like to go that feels peaceful. It may be outside, lying on a blanket in the sun. Maybe at night, it's looking up at the stars. You may have a special tree you like to sit by or a corner in your closet that makes you feel safe. As Michelle mentioned in an earlier devotion, counselors call this your "safe place." Go there, either in person or by shutting your eyes and picturing yourself there. Tell your Father you trust Him and know He will not forsake you. Ask Him to cover you with His peace.

Growing Stronger

Do you know someone who is often picked on, not included, or bullied? Choose one thing you can do to help this person not feel alone and also to experience knowing God as a stronghold or refuge. It doesn't have to be a huge thing, but bravely take one step.

12

Living at Peace

MICHELLE

Finally, brothers and sisters, rejoice! Strive for full restoration, encourage one another, be of one mind, live in peace. And the God of love and peace will be with you.

2 CORINTHIANS 13:11

If you'll remember from earlier readings in this book, I didn't grow up in a very peaceful home. I am the oldest of four kids, and after school, with no one around, we physically fought with each other. The contagious anger in our family materialized in punching, scratching, and saying hateful things. We escaped from sibling attacks to locked rooms for safety.

When I went to church camp, I experienced what it was like to live at peace with others. Adult mentors coached me on how to manage conflict in new ways. When I was younger, I said whatever came to my mind without considering how it might impact the person I was talking to. Through wise counsel, Father God imparted to me a vision of peaceful living in a home. When I got to college, I learned how to negotiate with roommates so we could all live at peace in the same space. Those discussions occurred over a meal where we took turns listening without interrupting, calmly explaining what we needed, and making requests for future change.

Recently, an author friend reminded me of the best way I've ever discovered to live at peace with others, even those I am meeting for the first time. Up until my midtwenties, when I was about to meet someone

I worried whether they would like me. I know now that these thoughts increased my social anxiety and made me more awkward than I already was. Now when I go into a situation, I confidently approach people for the first time with an attitude of *There you are.* I work at showing interest in them and note any similarities or differences we share. Using this approach makes others feel important and significant. This past month, I returned to my high school reunion and tried it out on classmates I knew and ones I'd probably never spoken to. It worked beautifully and I had a great time. As I left, it warmed my heart that the insecure girl I was had evolved into a vessel of God's love to those around me.

Experiencing Father God's Peace

Father, teach me what living in peace with others looks, feels, and acts like. Help me be a vessel of Your love so that others can experience peace around me, whether I live with them or am meeting them for the first time. Amen.

Growing Stronger

When you interact with people, see what it's like to focus on who they are instead of worrying about how you appear to them. Look for someone you don't know this week and take time to meet them and interact from a *There you are* approach.

13

Be at Peace

LYNN

"Be at peace with each other."

MARK 9:50

Confused, I listened to my teacher in our Christian school give his opinion on a passage of Scripture. What he said the verses meant and what I had been taught by my pastor at church were not the same. Not only did they not agree, they opposed each other. These differences made me wonder: *How could we all be studying the same Bible and have different views?*

We're not the only ones to wonder about believers and the differences that sometimes divide us. In Mark 9:38, the apostle John came to Jesus with this declaration: "'Teacher,' said John, 'we saw someone driving out demons in your name and we told him to stop, because he was not one of us.'" Jesus responded to John: "Do not stop him. For no one who does a miracle in my name can in the next moment say anything bad about me, for whoever is not against us is for us" (vv. 39–40).

Jesus showed His disciples what it can look like to be a peacemaker. Instead of looking for, pointing out, and arguing over what makes one believer different from another, Jesus said that if they are not against us (that is, if their beliefs align with Scripture), they are for us. He went on to end His teaching in this passage with this phrase: "Be at peace with each other" (Mark 9:50).

Our Father is a God of peace. He wants to bring His peace to people. Father God wants us to be people who not only have His peace within us but also people who bring His peace to others.

Experiencing Father God's Peace

Ask the Father to empower you to receive His peace in your life, to be a person who looks for ways to bring His peace into your world, and to become a person who is at peace with other people. When those around you look at you, do they see the Father's peace working in and through you? How could you share His peace in such a way that they might want it too?

You can also pray this prayer: Father, my peace, when I feel confused or want to argue with others about differences in how we believe, remind me of the words of Jesus: "Be at peace with each other." May I be at peace, carry Your peace, and be a peacemaker in my world. Amen.

Growing Stronger

Read Jesus's teaching in Mark 9:38–50. Read it with the Father filter, keeping in mind God's unconditional and perfect love for you. Read it thinking of Him being our peace. How can you experience God's peace to a greater degree in your life?

14

Peaceful Sleep

MICHELLE

In peace I will lie down and sleep, for you alone,
LORD, make me dwell in safety.

PSALM 4:8

*H*ow's your sleep?" is a common question counselors ask because of the impact lack of sleep can have on your physical and mental health. I have started sending younger and younger kids for sleep studies because even if they take something to fall asleep, like magnesium or melatonin, they have trouble staying asleep for seven to nine hours, barely meeting the minimum needed. Often our bodies struggle with sleep because they don't feel safe. Racing thoughts and stress can activate hyperarousal in our brains that bounces around in our bodies, making us exhausted but unable to rest.

Our Father wants us to sleep and promises to watch over us at night. He doesn't sleep or slumber (Psalm 121:4). Finding peaceful rest often begins with good sleep habits like going to bed and waking at consistent times, removing screens from your eyes thirty minutes before bedtime, maintaining simple routines like brushing your teeth, flossing, face washing, using night creams, or wearing retainers or night guards. I personally am learning to listen to my body and go to sleep in a certain time window to avoid activating my second wind by staying up late, thus making getting up in the morning difficult. And if you're still struggling to fall asleep, sometimes warming your body up can help trick it into feeling sleepy. You could try a hot drink, warm bath, heating pad, or an electric throw.

Once you are under the covers, it's a great time to tap into God's peace. Read a devotional, say a prayer, recite a Scripture, or play soothing Christian music. If you hum to the music, it's hard to think at all. Try it. Breathe in God's peace and breathe out any worries racing through your mind. If you need to, put a little notebook and writing tool by your bed so you can write down anything you need to remember, because the act of connecting your hands to your brain will slow your thoughts down.

Experiencing Father God's Peace

Father, help me experience Your peace at night when I need to rest. May I leave my worries in Your loving arms. Release my tight muscles so my body can relax, and help my nervous system to be calm. Help me remember that I am safe. I can rest knowing You are working while I sleep. Amen.

Growing Stronger

Select a helpful sleep habit from the ideas in today's reading and work on it this week.

15

When a Delete Leads to Peace

LYNN

On my bed I remember you; I think of you through the watches of the night. Because you are my help, I sing in the shadow of your wings. I cling to you; your right hand upholds me.

PSALM 63:6-8

It felt like I just couldn't help myself; I kept reading the text over and over. As I lay on my bed in the dark, I would read the message, experience the waves of pain, then lay my phone down. Several minutes later, I picked it up again. *Did they really say that? How could they have said something so hurtful?* Even though I knew I would experience fresh hurt each time I read it, like a tongue rolling over a toothache, I struggled to keep my hand off my phone.

Then I finally did it.

I deleted the text.

If I wouldn't stop myself from repeatedly reading it, the best thing I could do was get rid of it. Instead of remembering what they said, I, like the psalmist, needed to remember God is my help and will uphold me as I cling to Him.

Sometimes the best thing we can do to tap into God's peace is to get away from someone or something else. I wasn't experiencing the peace of God's word because I was upsetting myself with someone else's words. My actions barricaded the peace of God from reaching my heart.

If you've experienced a broken relationship or betrayal, going to social media (where people post their "happiness") can also block God's peace from reaching your heart. Delete the social media app from your device or at least unfollow or hide the person or people whose profiles keep your pain fresh or make it worse.

You may have a friendship or relationship that stirs up anxiety in your soul; maybe it's time to delete the relationship. Sometimes a delete is what we need to gain Father God's peace.

Finding His peace can be that easy . . . and that hard too.

Experiencing Father God's Peace

Is there an area of your life that is causing anxiety, sadness, or fear? Ask your Father to reveal to you if there is something you need to delete to help you to experience His peace.

Growing Stronger

Just as there are things we may need to delete to experience the God of peace, there are also tools we can incorporate into our lives to help us experience His peace. Do a search today for worship songs that speak of God's peace, and choose a song to listen to often over the next few days.

16

Sharing Words
of Peace

MICHELLE

Mercy, peace and love be yours in abundance.

JUDE 1:2

When you read the letters in the New Testament, you will notice a common theme in either the greeting or farewell. They wish each other intangible gifts like mercy, peace, and love. When I'm in my counseling role, I'm very aware of the energy I have in the room or online and how it impacts my clients. I think about their issues and pray about what they might need from their time with me. For those who are scattered, I direct them toward focus and intention. For those struggling with depression, I hold out hope for them that life can be different and bring energy when they seem lethargic. Can you imagine greeting an anxious person with chaos? Christian counselors work at creating an atmosphere of calm because we want to be vessels of God's peace in the midst of hard times.

I've also discovered that my days in the counseling office are often filled with more hope, joy, and peace than some of my days at home, as I speak hope, joy, and peace into the lives of others. That's because when we share Father God's peace, we experience His peace in our own minds and bodies. I went to a church camp and attended a church in high school where we passed the peace by saying, "Grace and peace be with you" and responding, "And with you also." I asked my young adult daughter if she would feel comfortable greeting her friends in this manner, and she gave me a firm no. But what if instead of saying, "Grace and peace to you," we approached people with a spirit of grace and peace? I've been trying that recently and I've discovered that as I engage with my family, friends, coworkers, and clients this way, I am less quick to judge, be offended, and get irritated with their mannerisms, behaviors, and what we often call *attitudes*. What would it be like to have a bad day, be frustrated, or feel irritated and be shown grace? How could you share God's peace with others in your life?

Experiencing Father God's Peace

Father, I not only want to live at peace with others as much as it depends on me (Romans 12:18), I want to become a vessel of peace in this difficult world. May Your grace and peace flow through me to others so that they may see Christ in me. In Jesus's name, amen.

Growing Stronger

Before interacting with people in your life, be intentional about approaching them with a spirit of grace and peace. Memorize Romans 12:18 to help you remember we are called to be at peace with others as much as it depends on us.

17

Got to Have It

LYNN

You, God, are my God, earnestly I seek you; I
thirst for you, my whole being longs for you, in a
dry and parched land where there is no water.

PSALM 63:1

*H*ave you ever hiked in a desert? My husband and I hike, but doing so in a place with soaring temperatures and no shade or water is not my favorite. I've never chewed on cotton balls, but I'm sure it feels similar to running out of water in a desert.

Like yearning for water in a desert, you and I were created to crave God. David described his desire for the Father in Psalm 63:1: "You, God, are my God, earnestly I seek you; I thirst for you, my whole being longs for you, in a dry and parched land where there is no water." David wrote this passage when he was in a desert and thirsty. He compares his thirst with his need for God.

Safe and stable or rocky and volatile, our definition of **love** begins to form even before we breathe our first breath. In the womb, our spirits sense peace or chaos. Strife or security. All the while, the Father is there. Forming us, creating us, lovingly putting the final touches on our image made in His. Yes, from our very beginning we are loved.

Soon after our birth, we begin to understand the difference between a sweet smile and a stern scowl. We learn to adjust our actions to receive what we need: love. We were created to crave human love, and we always will. Yet even deeper, we have always craved the Father's love.

And it is in *this* love—the perfect love that has been there from the beginning—that we can experience our Father's peace, know our worth, and be whole. "I will be fully satisfied as with the richest of foods; with singing lips my mouth will praise you" (Psalm 63:5).

Experiencing Father God's Peace

Below, describe your experience so far with love. Has it been peaceful? Painful? Nonexistent? If love has been peaceful, thank your Father. If it has not, speak to Him of your pain, and ask Him to help you experience Him filling your heart with His peace and love.

Growing Stronger

Read Psalm 63. Which phrases show that the psalmist experienced Father God's peace? Share in the space below.

18

Blessed with the Peace of God

MICHELLE

The LORD gives strength to his people; the LORD blesses his people with peace.

PSALM 29:11

I grew up with the belief we have to work hard for what we attain. Even gifts often seemed to come out of obligation or with strings attached, instead of being given simply because of love or because someone was being generous. While my earthly father struggled with generosity, our heavenly Father does not. He pours out His blessings on us. If you grew up like me, you may struggle with receiving. I forget God wants me to succeed. When we forget Father God's blessings, we leave Him out of the picture and become overwhelmed because we think it all depends on us. The pressure is too much for our human bodies to handle and it lets us know. Our hearts begin to race, we go to sleep and wake up with worry, and we find ourselves in bed as our immune systems crash.

What if you wholeheartedly believed you were blessed? Not because of who you are and what you do but because of who God is? How would that change the pressure you feel on the inside? Would it free you to let go of striving to be perfect? Could you allow yourself to rest even when there is so much to do? I challenge my counseling clients and myself weekly with these questions. Then I encourage them to dwell not on their weaknesses but on God's strength, believing He is for them!

Experiencing Father God's Peace

Listen to the song "Way Maker," performed by Leeland. (You can find it online or in your favorite music app.) Receive God's blessing as you focus on who He is today. Trust Father God to work on your behalf. Feel your load become lighter. You may want to lift your hands as you let go of your worries.

Growing Stronger

Pray the prayer of Jabez every chance you get until you have it memorized.

> *"Jabez cried out to the God of Israel, 'Oh, that you would bless me and enlarge my territory! Let your hand be with me, and keep me from harm so that I will be free from pain.' And God granted his request" (1 Chronicles 4:10).*

19

Wide Open

LYNN

I will be glad and rejoice in your love, for you saw my affliction and knew the anguish of my soul. You have not given me into the hands of the enemy but have set my feet in a spacious place.

PSALM 31:7-8

*D*on't do that. Bad girls do that.
Don't say that. Bad girls talk like that.

As a teen, it felt like the rules—spoken and unspoken—went on and on. I tried my best to know them all and follow them perfectly. Trying to get every action, every thought just right suffocated me. The tiny space of perfect behavior was a hard place to live. Many times, I wasn't quite sure who *I* was. Giving my all to be the best me others wanted me to be was exhausting. I wasn't sure how long I could keep it up. But what would happen if I failed? How harsh would the rejection be? I had bought into the lie that love is based on how I behaved, and this lie stole my peace.

Our enemy wants us to believe the Father's unconditional love—love that is free to all and free for all people—is not "free" at all. Satan speaks lies and wants us to believe we have to earn and repay Father God's love. Push, push . . . prove that you are worthy of His love.

Why is it important to the Enemy that we believe the lie of trying harder?

Because the pushing to prove I'm worthy of the Father's love actually pushes me from His love. Our enemy knows the power love brings into our lives. Unconditional love gives us the freedom to fulfill the potential

Father God poured into us when He created us. The devil doesn't want us to fulfill our potential because it will bring glory to God and joy to us, the ones our Father loves. Satan knows that if he can cause us to believe it is up to us to be lovable, he can push us right back to his prison of trying to be good enough. Romans 8 defines this as the law of sin and death. Satan's prison of wrestling and working for the approval and love of our Father keeps us away from the Father.

Experiencing Father God's Peace

Do you ever find yourself stressing about whether you've done something just right? Worrying if you've messed up too badly to be embraced? Ask Father God to help you more deeply understand what His unconditional love really looks like and free you from the prison of needing to be perfect.

Growing Stronger

Read 1 Corinthians 13. As you read the definition of love, think of how your Father is each of these attributes. What attributes mean the most to you right now? Share in the space below.

20

God Pleaser

MICHELLE

When people's lives please the LORD, even their
enemies are at peace with them.

PROVERBS 16:7 NLT

Whom do you want to please more than anyone else? As a Christian, I want to answer that question with "God, of course." But if I am honest, if that was truly the case I'd spend less time focused on achieving more, making money, shopping, and caring what others think about me and more time resting in God's presence and building His kingdom.

Father God is searching the earth for people whose main agenda is to please Him (2 Chronicles 16:9). He wants to strengthen them. He even promises to help them overcome their enemies. Solomon, the writer of Proverbs, was an Israelite king. His enemies were people and other countries. Today, our enemies are unseen. Ephesians 6:12 says, "For our struggle is not against flesh and blood, but against the rulers, against the authorities, against the powers of this dark world and against the spiritual forces of evil in the heavenly realms."

I have been fighting darkness for over twenty years. I've done this by treating people in an inpatient hospital for those struggling with severe trauma, in a group home for abused children, as a school crisis counselor, and in our counseling offices. People's enemies today are thoughts of death to the point where suicide seems like an option, self-hatred so extreme that someone would starve or cut themselves, loneliness and self-doubt after being betrayed by someone they love, and traumatic stress to the point it shuts a person's body down completely. Our Father has promised us victory and peace over these enemies. Victory over our mental health battles can begin when we choose to become God pleasers, knowing He is already pleased with us because of Jesus. When our battle cry becomes, "I desire to please God above all else," we find victory over fear, hopelessness, and loneliness, because He becomes our hope. Will you join me as a loved daughter of God and choose to please your heavenly Father above all else today?

Experiencing Father God's Peace

Father, thank You that Jesus makes us worthy. Help us to fully grasp Your love (Ephesians 3:18) and in response, may our lives revolve around pleasing You. Help us to remember that our enemies are not the things we see. Thank You that our victory is already won because Your Holy Spirit within us is greater than anyone or anything in our world (1 John 4:4)! Amen.

Growing Stronger

When my husband and I got engaged, I was intentional about doing little things to show him how much I loved him. List five ways you could demonstrate your love for your heavenly Father today.

1. _____
2. _____
3. _____
4. _____
5. _____

Provider

MEDITATION MATTERS

"Therefore I tell you, do not worry about your life, what you will eat or drink; or about your body, what you will wear. Is not life more than food, and the body more than clothes?"

MATTHEW 6:25

"Suppose one of you has a hundred sheep and loses one of them. Doesn't he leave the ninety-nine in the open country and go after the lost sheep until he finds it? And when he finds it, he joyfully puts it on his shoulders and goes home."

LUKE 15:4–6

But God demonstrates his own love for us in this: While we were still sinners, Christ died for us.

ROMANS 5:8

"But seek first his kingdom and his righteousness, and all these things will be given to you as well. Therefore do not worry about tomorrow, for tomorrow will worry about itself. Each day has enough trouble of its own."

MATTHEW 6:33–34

129

1

How Great Are You?

LYNN

At that time the disciples came to Jesus and asked,
"Who, then, is the greatest in the kingdom of heaven?"
He called a little child to him, and placed the child
among them. And he said: "Truly I tell you, unless you
change and become like little children, you will never
enter the kingdom of heaven. Therefore, whoever takes
the lowly position of this child is the greatest in the
kingdom of heaven."

MATTHEW 18:1-4

Who is greatest in the kingdom of heaven? the disciples asked Jesus. What kind of question is that?

Maybe the disciples were concerned they weren't measuring up to Jesus's expectations as disciples. Maybe they were afraid they wouldn't "make the cut," if there was one.

We can be pretty safe in saying that the disciples were not secure in Jesus's love for them.

To answer their question, Jesus called over a child. He placed the child among them and told His disciples to become like children.

Isn't this backward? Shouldn't His disciples be growing up? Becoming stronger and deeper in their understanding of Jesus's teachings? Yet Jesus told them that in order to become great, they needed to "change," or as translated in another version, "turn" (CSB). He told them to humble themselves—to not be proud or arrogant, thinking they already knew what they needed to know. He said instead to be like a child.

Why a child?
A child:

- trusts where their father goes and where he leads.
- does not worry. A child of a good father trusts their father completely.
- expects their father to provide for them and give them what they need.

In our lives, Father God can be trusted every day in every moment. He wants to lead us. Not only does He not begrudge us for coming to Him for help, but He also says this is the way to greatness in His kingdom.

What a gift Jesus gave His disciples, and you and I, when He made this clear: to be great in our Father's kingdom, which is like no other, we go to God for what we need. We come to Him with *all* of our needs, knowing He has been waiting for us to come to Him all along.

Experiencing Father God's Provision

Our Father, we thank You that becoming great in Your eyes is not difficult; it simply means coming to You. Amen.

Growing Stronger

There are several stories in the Bible of Jesus and little children. Read the following and think about what point Jesus is making in each one: Matthew 18:1–6, Mark 10:13–16, and Luke 18:15–17.

2

God Provides an Eternal Perspective

MICHELLE

"Therefore I tell you, do not worry about your
life, what you will eat or drink; or about your
body, what you will wear. Is not life more than
food, and the body more than clothes?"

MATTHEW 6:25

I've treated girls and women with body image struggles for over two decades. Some love the mirror! They love cultivating a wardrobe that impresses their peers and are often obsessed with working out and tracking every bite they eat. But they worry so much, it leads to anxiety, which leads to restricting their calories until their body isn't getting the food it needs. Sometimes their hunger and emotions intervene and they then overeat or binge. Both of these behaviors can lead to disordered eating. These young women feel good about themselves when the scales read a certain number and their clothes fit a certain way. But they become distressed if they lose control.

Other girls and women hate the image they see in the mirror. They focus on their flaws and work to hide their appearance, often avoiding cameras at all costs. They hate getting dressed in the morning because they wonder what else might not fit as they enter their closet. Often their self-loathing leads them to turn to food for comfort. With every pound they gain, they feel more helpless. They want to look and feel different but they can't seem to make it work no matter what diet or exercise plan they try. They notice other girls who they believe look good and wish they could trade places.

Father God has provided a way out of our obsession with our appearance and approach to food. Scripture reminds us He made us and we have value. His Word also teaches us that what happens here on earth isn't all that matters in the light of eternity. Our Father promises us glorious bodies in heaven (Philippians 3:21). What would it look like to see beyond just your physical appearance when you looked in the mirror? How could you train the thoughts in your head to center on more than just the physical image you see?

Our bodies are temples of the Holy Spirit and we are commanded to honor God with our bodies (1 Corinthians 6:20–21). No matter your current size, what would it look like for you to honor God with your body today?

Experiencing Father God's Provision

Father, help me focus on the good things about my earthly body. It works well, gets me places, houses the Holy Spirit in me, and allows me to glorify and serve You. Give me spiritual eyes to see beyond this world to what is eternal. In Jesus's name, amen.

Growing Stronger

Read Matthew 6:25–34. Put your name before each *therefore* and *your*. When you see the word *you*, substitute your name instead.

3

Love for the Wanderer

LYNN

"Suppose one of you has a hundred sheep and loses one of them. Doesn't he leave the ninety-nine in the open country and go after the lost sheep until he finds it? And when he finds it, he joyfully puts it on his shoulders and goes home. Then he calls his friends and neighbors together and says, 'Rejoice with me; I have found my lost sheep.' I tell you that in the same way there will be more rejoicing in heaven over one sinner who repents than over ninety-nine righteous persons who do not need to repent."

LUKE 15:4–7

I've experienced all types of being "lost."

Right after high school, I thought I knew my next steps. Yet, when I headed in that direction, doors seem to shut and peace was gone. What subject should I study? Should I move somewhere? Who should I date? In a fog, I looked and hoped for direction.

In Luke 15, Jesus tells three stories having to do with someone or something being lost: the lost sheep, the lost coin, and the lost son.

Luke 15:1–2 describes the scene of His storytelling this way: "Now the tax collectors and sinners were all gathering around to hear Jesus. But the Pharisees and the teachers of the law muttered, 'This man welcomes sinners and eats with them.'"

Jesus knew these people's thoughts and heard their mumbling. I can't help but think how irritated Jesus was that these teachers didn't understand who He was and why He had come. Instead of blasting these teachers, Jesus told a story. Reread His words above from Luke 15:4–7.

Jesus makes it clear: Father God is not ashamed of the wanderer. He doesn't try to hide the fact that she moved away from His care and the rest of the flock. The Father searches out the wanderer. He extends His staff to pull her off the cliff and out of the pit.

Then the Good Shepherd, a picture of Jesus, claims her. Hear what He calls her? *My* lost sheep. *Mine.* Even though she chose to wander, He still says, *She is mine.*

And He celebrates! *I* have found My sheep. And He does the same with you and me when we draw close and allow Him to care for us.

Experiencing Father God's Provision

Where does the shepherd put the sheep that had been lost?

How does the shepherd feel once he's found the lost sheep?

Growing Stronger

When the shepherd in Jesus's story found his sheep, he put her across his shoulders to carry her home. Maybe she got hurt while she was away. In the Old Testament, God is pictured as a shepherd as well. Read Isaiah 40:11. Where does the Shepherd carry you?

4

Give It to Me Now

LYNN

Jesus continued: "There was a man who had two sons. The younger one said to his father, 'Father, give me my share of the estate.' So he divided his property between them."

LUKE 15:11–12

When have you wanted something but it wasn't time for it yet? Maybe it's your driver's license. You want to go where you want when you want. And yet, it's not time. If your parents were to give you their keys without you having enough experience behind the wheel, it could be deadly for both you and others.

In the parable in Luke 15 of the lost son—which is sometimes called the parable of the running father—the younger son wants his share of his father's estate. But it's not time yet. The son's request is strange, and might I add, rude. An inheritance is given *after* a parent dies. His father is obviously still living. With his request, the son is telling the father he values his father's stuff more than their relationship.

The loving father doesn't argue with his son and what the son wants. He knows his son is not ready for this level of responsibility. He also knows his son is unwilling to listen to him. The father's words may not be received and instead could create resentment and bitterness in his son's heart. The father doesn't want that. He wants a loving relationship with his son.

Out of love, the selfless father provides the selfish desires of his son. He holds his thoughts and holds in his hurt. He watches his son pack and he watches him go. The father doesn't try to talk him out of going. In love, the father releases his son to go.

Experiencing Father God's Provision

Father God has set in place protection out of His love for us. Like the son, we may not like our Father's provision, but unlike the son, we can be wise and choose to adhere to His loving wisdom. Write about an area of provision and/or protection that feels uncomfortable or restrictive to you right now.

_____

_____

_____

_____

_____

_____

_____

_____

_____

_____

_____

Growing Stronger

Read Jesus's entire parable about this son and father in Luke 15:11–32.

5

Run to the Father

LYNN

> *"Not long after that, the younger son got together
> all he had, set off for a distant country and there
> squandered his wealth in wild living . . . When
> he came to his senses, he said, 'How many of my
> father's hired servants have food to spare, and
> here I am starving to death! I will set out and go
> back to my father and say to him: Father, I have
> sinned against heaven and against you.'"*

LUKE 15:13, 17–18

If there is one thing that can make me mad, it's when someone says, "I told you so." There's nothing quite like having someone rub a mistake in your face.

The father in the parable of the running father had every reason to say, "I told you so" when his son came home, yet he didn't.

The father had provided his son with what the son wanted even though it wasn't for his best. The father not only let the son go, but once he was gone, the father didn't chase him down. He allowed whatever would happen to happen. The father allowed tough circumstances to bring his son "to his senses."

A good father doesn't intervene at the wrong times. Pure love let the son go, leaving the father brokenhearted. The father got out of the way so his son could learn his way. If the father had begged the son to stay or come home, the son may have remained the selfish person he was. The son wouldn't have seen what his selfishness had made him become, like he did when he was stuck feeding pigs (Luke 15:15–16).

Allowing the son to suffer didn't make the father a bad father; it made him a wise and loving father. He was willing to let his son go so the son could become who he was meant to be. The father let the son go so the son could experience all the blessings of being deeply and unconditionally loved once he returned.

Experiencing Father God's Provision

Our loving heavenly Father sometimes lets us go our own way so that we can learn how difficult it is being on our own. When we return to Him, our experience of His blessings becomes more meaningful because of our time away. Father God knows what we need when we need it.

Is there an area of your life where you are struggling, wanting to run away from your Father's loving protection? Ask Him to reveal to you what is driving you to run. Write any answer(s) you receive on the lines below.

Growing Stronger

Find and listen to the song "Run to the Father" by Cody Carnes. Do you feel any particular emotion as you listen?

6

When God Ran

LYNN

"I am no longer worthy to be called your son;
make me like one of your hired servants."

LUKE 15:19

*A*s the son sets off for home, he prepares a speech for his father: "'I'm going back to my father. I'll say to him, Father, I've sinned against God, I've sinned before you; I don't deserve to be called your son. Take me on as a hired hand.' He got right up and went home to his father" (Luke 15:18–19 MSG).

The son failed to see and understand his father's love; his words reveal this. He was prepared to say, "I am no longer worthy." He doesn't get that he is unconditionally loved. He doesn't understand the love of a father that sees beyond past choices and character flaws.

Yet we see in the story that the son is worth *everything* to the father. "So he got up and went to his father. But while he was still a long way off, his father saw him and was filled with compassion for him; he ran to his son, threw his arms around him and kissed him" (Luke 15:20).

What kind of father feels compassion, of all things, for a child who has treated him the way this son has?

A father who loves purely.

A father who believes his child is worthy of love, even when the world wants that child to think differently.

A father whose love is not built upon how he is treated, but who loves with arms wide open.

Like the father in the story, when we are not close to Father God,

PROVIDER

when we are not in His arms or near enough to hear His voice, our Father is looking for us. He is anticipating that we will come (2 Chronicles 16:9).

In the story, all it took was for the son who had chosen to leave to show he wanted to return. With all he had, the father showed the son he wanted him to return as well. The father ran, embraced, and kissed him. He didn't wait for the son to say the right words. He didn't even wait for the son to say he was sorry. His father acted, demonstrating perfect love. The father was happy to have his son home.

Experiencing Father God's Provision

In ancient Israel, it was inappropriate for an adult man to run because to do so he would have had to pull up his tunic, which was long like a dress. In this time period it was "humiliating and shameful for a man to show his bare legs."* Why do you think, when Jesus told this story, He had the father run to the son who was coming home? Write your thoughts in the space below.

Growing Stronger

Look up Rembrandt's painting *The Return of the Prodigal Son*. What observations do you make concerning the father? The son? Those looking on?

---

* Matthew Williams, "The Prodigal Son's Father Shouldn't Have Run!" *Biola Magazine*, May 31, 2010, https://www.biola.edu/blogs/biola-magazine /2010/the-prodigal-sons-father-shouldnt-have-run.

1

But . . .

LYNN

"But the father said to his servants, 'Quick! Bring the best robe and put it on him. Put a ring on his finger and sandals on his feet.'"

LUKE 15:22

Whenever I read the word **but**, I pay close attention, because whatever comes after this word is more important than what was said before. According to Merriam-Webster's, *but* means "on the contrary." The word *but* nullifies, or wipes out, whatever was said before it.

Say you're having an argument with a friend. She asks for your forgiveness. You reply, "I forgive you, but . . ." You go on to tell her how she hurt you. Are you really forgiving her? Or are you looking for the opportunity to tell her why you're still mad and how much pain she caused?

Well, this "but" in Luke 15:22 is the best kind! The son has just said, "Father, I have sinned against heaven and against you. I am no longer worthy to be called your son" (v. 21). The next verse says, "But the father said to his servants, 'Quick! Bring the best robe and put it on him. Put a ring on his finger and sandals on his feet'" (v. 22).

This *but* means that the father is still moving, excited to carry out his plan of restoring his son. He doesn't need to hear the son's words because he already has his reply ready. What the son has said doesn't affect the love the father is ready to shower on his son. "Bring on the best of what I have" is all the father wants to say or do!

The father backed up his words of love with actions of love—his gifts of the best robe and the family ring. These gifts are outward signs from the father telling everyone, "My son is welcomed back into the family." The father was sending a clear sign that his son should be treated with love and forgiveness.

Experiencing Father God's Provision

Do you remember a time when you experienced love and forgiveness that you didn't "deserve"? Explain this situation below.

_____

_____

_____

_____

_____

_____

_____

_____

_____

_____

_____

_____

Growing Stronger

Read Luke 15:1–2. Who was Jesus specifically telling the story of the lost son to? Why do you think He told it to this crowd?

8

Father of the Second Chance

LYNN

"Bring the fattened calf and kill it. Let's have a feast and celebrate. For this son of mine was dead and is alive again; he was lost and is found." So they began to celebrate.

LUKE 15:23–24

The father and the son never had one of *those* conversations. At our house when our kids were growing up, those conversations—where you found out just how much trouble you were actually in—were held in the office. Not so with the lost son's father. His father doesn't get off his chest all the son had cost him, using weighted words to make him feel guilty or ashamed.

Nor does the father replay the day the son was demanding and left; the father didn't keep score or a record of the son's previous wrongs.

In fact, before the father even knew why the son was coming, he was running toward the son. He didn't wait for the son to get to him.

Even after all the son had done, the father withholds nothing; instead, he pours out on his child the best of all he has. The father doesn't wait to hear the son's story or feel the need to tell his own. He moves straight to celebrating. He does not withhold anything even though his son took what he could and did as he pleased. He doesn't wait to see if the son's actions changed, showing he really is sorry. The father just begins the party!

Through this story, Jesus shows us that Father God is the Father of the second chance. He proved it when He provided the same love for you and me. "But God demonstrates his own love for us in this: While we were still sinners, Christ died for us" (Romans 5:8). Jesus did not come for us once we got it together, begged, and came back to Him. No, "while we were still sinners," He came for us. Even then, Father God demonstrated His love by sending His Son, Jesus, to sacrifice His life for us.

Our Father's love is never-ending. He will be there, ready to shower it upon you today, tomorrow, and all the days that follow.

Experiencing Father God's Provision

Thank the Father for providing His love and forgiveness to you today. If you would like a prompt, begin by saying, "Father, thank You for loving me so much that You ran to me even when I was not moving toward You."

Growing Stronger

Read Romans 5:6–11. Reflect for a moment on our "before and after." What was life like before Christ came for us, and what is it like after?

9

Only Good Is Coming Out

LYNN

"A good man brings good things out of the good stored up in his heart, and an evil man brings evil things out of the evil stored up in his heart. For the mouth speaks what the heart is full of."

LUKE 6:45

*H*ave you ever gotten in a fight with a sibling or a friend and said something you really wish you hadn't? It was so mean or ugly, you wondered, *Where did that come from?* "You always look for the worst," "You never take my side," and "I'll never trust you again" are examples of painful words that have exploded from my lips as the pounding of my sinful heart drowned out any reasoning in my mind. I've heard it said that what is stored up in a person's heart comes out under pressure. I believe it because I have experienced it.

Luke 6:45 puts it this way: "What you say flows from what is in your heart" (NLT).

In the story of the lost son in Luke 15, what flowed from the father's heart was unconditional love, not reprimanding, name-calling, or judging. He made it clear that he was still *for* his child. The father provided a clean slate and a pathway back to a relationship.

As the father continued his conversation with others about his son, he only built the son up. He didn't embarrass his son in front of others or talk badly about him behind his back. The forgiveness he provided was real and authentic.

God provides this same mercy if we pursue a relationship with Him:

"For as high as the heavens are above the earth, so great is his love for those who fear him; as far as the east is from the west, so far has he removed our transgressions from us. As a father has compassion on his children, so the LORD has compassion on those who fear him; for he knows how we are formed, he remembers that we are dust" (Psalm 103:11–14).

When our Father provides forgiveness, the past is over. He won't remind you of past sins if you fail in the same way tomorrow. Your heavenly Father has made this promise: "Because of the LORD's great love we are not consumed, for his compassions never fail. They are new every morning; great is your faithfulness" (Lamentations 3:22–23).

Experiencing Father God's Provision

Sit for a moment and reflect, thinking about how our Father removes our sin from us completely. How is your life different, or how might it be different, knowing the heavenly Father removes our sin from us totally?

Growing Stronger

Looking at Psalm 103:11–14, how would you describe in your own words, "as far as the east is from the west, so far has he removed our transgressions from us"?

10

God Provides His Way

MICHELLE

"If that is how God clothes the grass of the field,
which is here today and tomorrow is thrown into
the furnace, will he not much more clothe you—
you of little faith?"

MATTHEW 6:30

When I grow up, I'm going to be successful and make a lot of money so I never feel less than anyone else again." I made this vow when I was in middle school. Everything I did in high school moved toward that goal. My friends seemed to have more money than my family did. When I wanted something, I often heard, "Sorry, we can't afford that. You are one of four kids." In high school, I decided to work hard so I would get scholarships, go to a great school, and someday drive a really nice car, unlike the junker I could barely afford. In college, I struggled with not being resentful of other girls who had huge allowances and unlimited access to their parents' credit cards. They didn't have to think about a budget and working all summer to make enough to live on during the year.

Approaching life from a scarcity mindset, I made an ungodly vow to myself to pursue wealth so I'd never have to worry about money again. Reading passages like Matthew 6 convicted me that it wasn't my bank account that was the problem but my mindset. In a world that promises instant wealth, money leading to happiness, and financial security based on our own wise choices, learning to rely on Father God to provide requires a never-ending battle of the mind. Weapons we can use to win this war include reminding ourselves of times the Father miraculously provided for His people in the Bible, recording moments when God provided for us, and reviewing them when we are anxious.

Practicing contentment is a tool I learned from my sister Melissa Spoelstra. For a season, we had bracelets with the word **content** on them. Each time we complained, we switched the arm the bracelet was on and chose three things we were grateful for. At first, my bracelet moved often, but over time I trained my brain to focus on the good I had instead of worrying about circumstances beyond my control.

Experiencing Father God's Provision

Father, I want to be a woman of faith, trusting You alone for my daily bread (Luke 11:3). In the Old Testament, You are called Jehovah Jireh, my provider. May my security be rooted in the person of who You are and not the amount in my bank account. Amen.

Growing Stronger

Are you looking toward your own gifts, talents, and hard work to provide for you, or to God? Take a sheet of paper and fold it in half. On the left side, write how relying solely on yourself would look and feel. On the right side, write what it would look and feel like to trust God daily.

11

God Provides His Kingdom

MICHELLE

*"But seek first his kingdom and his righteousness,
and all these things will be given to you as well.
Therefore do not worry about tomorrow, for
tomorrow will worry about itself. Each day has
enough trouble of its own."*

MATTHEW 6:33–34

Y ou keep talking about the 'kingdom,' but whose kingdom are you building?" My life coach recently asked me this question during our monthly session. When I was a high school counselor, I observed and intervened in lots of "kingdoms" where something in common bound students together. If you excelled and were well-liked in one of these kingdoms, you might be chosen as a leader. Some of these leaders held their status through fear, intimidation, and the threat of humiliation if you weren't loyal at all costs.

While these "kingdoms" make us feel included or give us something to strive for, they don't last. Your inclusion in them can change. When you move, enter the workforce, or go off to college, high school "kingdoms" fade away and you have to start over.

Focusing on earthly kingdoms also creates a lot of stress in our lives. We are tempted to feel rejected when we see friends' posts or hear about a fun party we weren't invited to. We wonder if we did something wrong or if there is something wrong with us to explain why we weren't included.

Your heavenly Father offers you a kingdom that's all-inclusive and lasts forever. You enter His kingdom by trusting in Jesus, and it's yours no matter your background, your interests, or how talented or well-liked you are. All are welcome and you are accepted as you are. In our Father's kingdom change occurs not because we try harder but because we connect with Him, let ourselves be loved, and allow His Spirit to work in and through us. We can relax because Father God has promised that if we seek His kingdom, He will take care of everything else.

Experiencing Father God's Provision

What kingdoms have had your focus lately? Those on earth or God's? Write out a description of what it could look like to have a day focused on God's kingdom. How would your day start? What would you think about first thing in the morning? As you went to school? While you sat in class? On your way home from school or work? While doing your homework? When you looked at social media? When you got in bed? Would you focus on belonging to the kingdoms of this world or building His eternal, all-embracing one? Share about your day in the lines below.

Growing Stronger

Read Matthew 6:25–34 for the third time. Ponder how you would be less anxious if you focused on God's kingdom instead of all the kingdoms of this world.

12

God Provides Good Things

MICHELLE

"If you, then, though you are evil, know how to give good gifts to your children, how much more will your Father in heaven give good gifts to those who ask him!"

MATTHEW 7:11

Earthly parents often wish they could give their kids more than they are able. They delight in being able to say yes when their children make a request. Healthy parents desire to make things easier for their children to attain success.

In college, I often heard that we need to seek God's face as much as we ask for His hands. While this idea is well intentioned, I sometimes I think teachings like this make us feel guilty for coming to God with our wants and needs. God tells us to ask and we will receive, but He does have some qualifiers. We are to do so seeking first His kingdom (Matthew 6:33).

What gifts would you like to receive from God? As I talked with a group of college women this week, they listed self-discipline/control, discernment, wisdom, direction, patience to wait on God's timing, and the strength to resist temptation. These character qualities all take time to develop, but based on what God says in His Word, they are all possible. I once heard Shelley Giglio, the cofounder of the large Passion conferences for college-aged attendees, share that she has prayed for wisdom every day of her life since she was young. This is a prayer He is happy to answer! James 1:5 tells us God has promised to answer the prayer for wisdom with a yes! Just as loving earthly parents love to bless their kids with gifts, Father God delights in being our source of both spiritual gifts we cannot see as well as many that we can.

Experiencing Father God's Provision

Make a list of gifts you desire from God. Choose one to pray for daily for an extended period of time.

Growing Stronger

Read Psalm 37:4–5. What must we do in order for God to give us the desires of our heart? Share on the lines below.

13

God Provides Discernment

MICHELLE

"So give Your servant an understanding heart to judge Your people to discern between good and evil. For who is able to judge this great people of Yours?"

1 KINGS 3:9 NASB

I asked several college students, "What do you need God to provide for you in this stage of your life?" Two answers they all had in common were wisdom and discernment. When I was a youth minister, I taught my students that wisdom means applying the Word of God in your life as the Holy Spirit guides you. Wisdom also involves learning from your mistakes or, better yet, learning from the mistakes of others who have already walked where you're headed. I have constantly sought out older mentors in my life for both spiritual and professional reasons because I would rather learn from their missteps than experience the consequences of my own.

Discernment involves knowledge and wisdom but also involves an additional component of being highly tuned in to God's Spirit, learning to read and understand people, and trusting your God-given instincts when you sense trouble. One of my most difficult experiences that still affects me today occurred because I ignored what God had revealed to me regarding good and evil and trusted someone to protect me who couldn't. Satan is identified in Revelation 12:9 as the deceiver. Seeking discernment from God can protect us from the devil's traps.

Experiencing Father God's Provision

Father, I need Your discernment to choose wisely each day. Open up opportunities for me to discover people whose wisdom I need to learn from, whether in person or through their teachings. Give me the courage to seek out those who are wise and ask for their time and input. Thank You for giving us the ability to understand good and evil by knowing Your Word. Amen.

Growing Stronger

Meditate on and memorize Psalm 119:66: "Teach me knowledge and good judgment, for I trust your commands."

14

God Provides Patience

MICHELLE

But the Holy Spirit produces this kind of fruit in our lives: love, joy, peace, patience, kindness, goodness, faithfulness, gentleness, and self-control. There is no law against these things!

GALATIANS 5:22–23 NLT

One thing I've always struggled with but tend to avoid praying for is patience. I am very much an "I want it now" kind of gal. When I was in high school, I couldn't wait to graduate and go to college. When I was in college, I couldn't wait to become a minister and counselor. When I was a single adult, I wondered why it was taking so long for me to get married and have kids. When I got married at thirty-two, I wanted to be pregnant as soon as we started trying, but I struggled with infertility. When I signed a contract with my publishing agent, I wanted a book contract right away.

Christian friends who already had what I longed for would often talk about "God's timing." I wanted to roll my eyes. I felt restless when hearing sermons about "waiting on the Lord." I longed for His favor on my life sooner.

I can see now the tapestry God was weaving over the decades, working even those difficult seasons of waiting for my good (Romans 8:28). I wish I could assure you that waiting on God gets easier. What I do know for certain is that wrestling with your heart's desires and trusting in God instead of your own understanding (Proverbs 3:5–6) is so much better than becoming hopeless and miserable.

Experiencing Father God's Provision

Father, You know what my heart longs for and how desperate I am for You to answer my prayers. Help me to wait patiently and trust Your timing. Help me to remember that Your plans include a hope and a future for me (Jeremiah 29:11). If I'm holding on to any desires that are my own instead of yours, or come from my wanting what You've given to someone else that's not meant for me, give me the courage to let go of them and comfort me as I grieve the loss of a dream I've longed for. In Jesus's name, amen.

Growing Stronger

If you're in a time of waiting, do the next right thing instead of letting your frustration immobilize you. Research your options. Talk to Christians walking with the Lord who've been where you are. Ask questions and listen as they share God's faithfulness as a source of encouragement. Ask people to pray alongside you for Father God to give you the desires of your heart as you delight in Him (Psalm 37:4).

15

God Provides Help with Self-Control

MICHELLE

For this very reason, make every effort to add to your faith goodness; and to goodness, knowledge; and to knowledge, self-control; and to self-control, perserverance; and to perseverance, godliness.

2 PETER 1:5–6

If you ever struggle with pride, feeling like you've got it all together, take just a few minutes and inventory the areas of your life where you lack self-control. When I talk with students and young adults, they lament over time and energy demands of establishing an independent life. One hundred and sixty-eight hours in a week doesn't seem to be enough time for getting prescriptions filled, creating great housekeeping habits, managing money, trying to stay healthy without home-cooked meals and an exercise class, and setting aside time to pray, read their Bible, and maybe journal a little. Some have become anxious due to what seems like impossible demands and share that they are tempted to give up on living balanced, healthy lives. Our internal critics often kick in, calling us names like lazy or unmotivated. Feeling hopeless can lead to diversions like partying with friends, bingeing a television series, gaming for hours, or lying in bed scrolling and surfing.

If you over-relate to lacking self-control, hold on to hope. God has provided an ever-present helper (John 14:16). The Holy Spirit empowers us with self-discipline (2 Timothy 1:7), enabling us to resist distraction and complete unappealing but necessary tasks. Experiencing the fruit of self-control in our lives rewards us with improved mental health, physical strength and endurance, and more satisfying relationships.

Experiencing Father God's Provision

Father, I am trusting You to produce self-control in my life through the indwelling of Your Holy Spirit. Empower me to resist the temptation of distraction. Help me to make small changes that lead to bigger victories. In Jesus's name, amen.

Growing Stronger

Look up what is involved in creating a SMART goal. Choose only one aspect of your life where you lack self-control and create a plan for doing something hard. Start simple. You might attempt doing something for the first time, or you might rebuild a lost habit like flossing your teeth once a day, studying a minimum of one hour before a test, designating a specific time each month to look at your finances, or spending at least two minutes sitting quietly before the Lord. If you need some extra help, ask someone to pray for you or hold you accountable. If you need encouragement, read a book, listen to a podcast or audiobook, or watch a video teaching on habit building. I suggest Jordan Raynor's book *Redeeming Your Time*, which you can also find as a video teaching on YouTube.

16

God Provides Others to Hold Our Hands

MICHELLE

So it came about when Moses held his hand up, that Israel prevailed, and when he let his hand down, Amalek prevailed. But Moses' hands were heavy. Then they took a stone and put it under him, and he sat on it; and Aaron and Hur supported his hands, one on one side and one on the other. Thus his hands were steady until the sun set.

EXODUS 17:11–12 NASB

I would crash and burn without community," my college-aged niece shared with me recently.

Being a Christ follower in a world that frequently sees Christians in a negative light is tough. I often describe it to parents of teens in public schools as trying to canoe upstream with only one paddle. We need people in our boat to help us keep it moving and to row for us when we get tired.

My niece has struggled with social anxiety and knows how hard it is to find community. Walking into a new church takes courage. Attending a service and talking to someone you don't know requires vulnerability and a willingness to be known. Showing up for the first time for small group Bible study or a life group feels awkward. Walking into the unknown requires bravery.

The key ingredient for meaningful connection and community is time. Best friends aren't created in a week and neither are church families. Showing up Sunday after Sunday changes what once felt like a strange worship service into your church home. That person you barely knew when you first started going becomes someone whose face lights up when you walk into the room. As you share life together, that small group of strangers becomes your lifeline of closest confidants who pray with and for you and miraculously know to check on you when you've had the worst week ever.

Experiencing Father God's Provision

Make a list of Christians who've held up your hands when life was hard. Thank Father God for His vessels of love in your life.

Growing Stronger

If you're in a faith community, be on the lookout for someone new and take the first step of including them by introducing yourself and being curious about them. If you aren't in community at all, make a list of three churches to visit and talk to at least one person, fill out a visitor form, or visit their connection desk. If you are a church attender only, visit small groups until you find one that works for you, start your own, or volunteer in some area of service where you can get to know others.

17

God Provides Others to Strengthen Our Prayers

MICHELLE

"Again, truly I tell you that if two of you on earth agree about anything they ask for, it will be done for them by my Father in heaven."

MATTHEW 18:19

*H*ave you ever felt like your prayers were futile? I've experienced times in my life when I didn't even have the words to pray. In moments like these, I've often called a friend, gone up for prayer at the altar of a church, or even asked a woman I trusted or knew to place her hands on me and pray. I'll never forget when I was in college, I began having vivid dreams of holding a baby; then the baby's hands turned into claws that choked me, and I woke up gasping for air. That same morning, I was volunteering for Louie Giglio's ministry as a receptionist and he asked me if something was wrong. He felt I seemed "off." Tears leaked down my cheeks as I recounted how much sleep I was losing and the dream that kept reoccurring. He asked if he could pray for me and invited another volunteer to join him in his office. They placed their hands on me and began prayers of spiritual warfare, calling out for God's protection, and then spoke Scriptures claiming God's promises of rest and peace while I slept. Before I returned to my desk, they asked what time I usually went to bed and committed to pray for me at that time. How do you think I slept that night and the nights that followed? I woke up the next day well rested, rejoicing in answered prayers and grateful for his spiritual discernment. To this day, that nightmare has never haunted me again.

Who could you trust to pray for you when you feel like you are in a spiritual battle? Does your church have a prayer ministry? I love praying with and for my clients at the end of our counseling sessions, summarizing our conversation. When we've run out of time, I've sent them a voice prayer. Recently, I've sent voice prayers by text or through social media message systems so that friends across the country can hear my prayers spoken for them.

The next time someone shares their struggle with you, you might stop then and pray with and for them. You might want to follow up in the near future actually speaking or writing out a prayer for their specific need.

Experiencing Father God's Provision

Father, I confess I am foolish in my independence. I think I can handle things by myself. Give me the courage to ask and receive help when I need it. In Jesus's name, amen.

Growing Stronger

Ask someone to pray for and with you in person this week. Write a few sentences of what that experience was like for you.

_____

_____

_____

_____

18

How It Really Went Down

LYNN

Now the serpent was more crafty than any of the wild animals the Lord God had made. He said to the woman, "Did God really say, 'You must not eat from any tree in the garden'?"

GENESIS 3:1

What if the whole story of Adam and Eve was available in audio format, with the real characters reading their lines?

Can you hear Satan's voice? "Did God *really say* . . ." He digs the dirt of Eve's mind to plant seeds of doubt about Abba Father's goodness.

Satan's been targeting our hearts, the hearts of God's daughters, from the very beginning. We know Eve couldn't have had daddy issues. Her Father God was perfect! Yet the Enemy planted uncertainty in her heart about her heavenly Father's ability to care for her. Satan's question seems to have caused Eve to distrust God's love and the purity of His motives. When we experience distrust and doubt, anxiety follows, quickly creating a desire to control and fix the situation ourselves. We take the situation into our own hands.

Can you hear Eve's voice as she responds: "But God did say, 'You must not eat fruit from the tree that is in the middle of the garden, and you must not touch it, or you will die'" (Genesis 3:3). One part, "and you must not touch it," Eve added; God never said, "And you must not touch

PROVIDER

164

it." Open your Bible and read Genesis 2:17. Their Father God only gives a loving warning to provide for their protection.

The Enemy will attempt to use this same ancient strategy to manifest anxiety in you. He will try to entice you to not trust God with your needs and wants. He will try to confuse you, leading you to distrust Father God's goodness. Because the Enemy works so hard to deceive us, we need to read and study the Bible, picking up God's actual Word and experiencing it for ourselves. Because if we don't know what's in the Bible, we won't know when someone has twisted its words.

Experiencing Father God's Provision

Unlike Eve, you and I have the ability to read for ourselves God's actual Word. If you haven't started taking the extra step of doing the "Growing Stronger" section each day, it's not too late to start and learn more about your Father for yourself.

Growing Stronger

Read Genesis 2 and 3 so you can know exactly how the story went down. In Genesis 2:15–17 and Genesis 3:1, how do the words of God and the words of the serpent differ?

19

Where Are You?

LYNN

But the Lord God called to the man, "Where are you?"

GENESIS 3:9

If we listened to an audio version of the Bible and it was read by God, what would His tone be as He called to Adam and Eve, "Where are you?" (Genesis 3:9). Based on our experiences in life with others in authority, we may automatically attach a negative tone to that question.

Interpreting a person's tone when reading written words like a text is tricky. When trying to understand, we want to consider the person's character, assume the best, and listen to their choice of words.

Here in the garden, the Father chose a question. *Where are you?*

Except for the day when His Son died for our sins, this day in Eden is where I most clearly see the nature of His heart. Father God doesn't focus on Himself and all He's lost in the brief moment when Eve sinned and turned from Him. Instead, His loving heart calls out, "Where are you?" Our Father invites conversation instead of pointing out condemnation.

Father God invites us into conversation over and over again; two-way communication is the gateway to relationship. Communication is saying, "Talk. I want to hear what you have to say. I'm listening." In Isaiah 1:18, God says, "Come now, let us settle the matter. Though your sins are like scarlet, they shall be as white as snow; though they are red as crimson, they shall be like wool."

This verse teaches me that our Father is approachable and we can pour out all of our emotions before Him.

I used to believe if my feelings were negative, I shouldn't express them. I transferred this thinking to my relationship with God. I didn't feel the freedom to tell Him how I truly felt when I was hurt, mad, or disappointed.

Now I know I was wrong.

In this first story of His relationship with those He created, can you almost hear the longing for a relationship in His voice as He comes into the garden to find Adam and Eve? "Where are you?" He opens the door for dialogue.

Even when the relationship has suffered so much loss, there is Father God, reaching out in love for conversation, to provide for their needs, and to protect them from hurting themselves further.

Experiencing Father God's Provision

When you read or heard the story of Genesis 3, how did you interpret God's response in light of Adam and Eve's sin? Write out a commitment to trust in His unconditional love for you even when you aren't able to audibly hear His voice.

Growing Stronger

Choose one of the Meditation Matters verses for this section. Make a point to refer back to it more than once today, reminding your heart that Father God provides for you.

20

God Is Our Defender

MICHELLE

The LORD is my strength and my defense; he has
become my salvation. He is my God, and I will
praise him, my father's God, and I will exalt him.

EXODUS 15:2

You could let God defend you," Gail, my mentor and counselor in college, said when I sought her wisdom in a situation where I felt another person had misunderstood who I was and my heart in a ministry role. I grew up in a home where I received a lot of criticism. Dinner table conversations could turn into someone being made fun of, and when the offender was confronted about hurting someone's feelings, they'd say, "I was just kidding." As I got older, anytime I felt misunderstood, I wanted to correct that person's view of me and defend myself. I unconsciously equipped myself to use words as a defense by becoming an award-winning debater in high school. Even today, when I occasionally interact on social media in a professional group, I encounter someone who chooses to misread my motives, and I have to stop myself from continuing the futile conversation even if it means I don't get the last word.

"How could God defend me?" I asked Gail. She went on to share that God had way more control over another believer's mind, heart, and perceptions than I did. If unity was needed, God could highlight my strengths and convince them my motives were pure better than I ever could. If I didn't let some things go, I was going to waste a lot of energy trying to convince people to see me clearly. She also pointed out that people bring their own life lenses to a situation. Sometimes in life when someone doesn't like us, it's not because of who we are but because of their perspective, which has been influenced by past experiences and encounters. When we trust Father God to be our defender, we experience freedom from the impossibility of trying to make everyone like us.

Experiencing Father God's Provision

Father, defend me when someone chooses to attack my character. Give me wisdom and discernment to know when I need to reach out and attempt to make peace and when I need to trust You to be my Defender, letting go instead of insisting on having the last word. Protect me from reacting to things I hear secondhand from others. Help me to walk confidently, knowing that while I do mess up, I am Your child whom You delight in (Psalm 149:4). Surround me with others who see me through Your eyes. Amen.

Growing Stronger

Meditate on or memorize Psalm 55:22: "Leave your troubles with the LORD, and he will defend you; he never lets honest people be defeated" (GNT).

Presence

MEDITATION MATTERS

Those who know your name trust in you, for you, LORD, have never forsaken those who seek you.

PSALM 9:10

May your unfailing love be with us, LORD, even as we put our hope in you.

PSALM 33:22

You hem me in behind and before, and you lay your hand upon me.

PSALM 139:5

The LORD your God is with you, the Mighty Warrior who saves. He will take great delight in you; in his love he will no longer rebuke you, but will rejoice over you with singing.

ZEPHANIAH 3:17

1

Preparing Me

LYNN

For you, God, tested us; you refined us like silver.
You brought us into prison and laid burdens on
our backs. You let people ride over our heads; we
went through fire and water, but you brought us
to a place of abundance.

PSALM 66:10–12

*H*ave you ever wondered, *Where are You, God?* Wave after wave of "hard" kept coming into your life and now you haven't felt God close by for a long time. When trouble comes into my life, I can experience doubt, asking myself, *Is this worth it?* At times my mind has said to me, *Is God even real?*

When I was younger, I wouldn't tell anyone about these doubts. I thought my doubts meant I was weird or something was wrong with me. Possibly the doubts even meant I wasn't really a Christ follower.

But I have learned just the opposite. Sometimes thoughts of doubt come when I'm close to experiencing something new with God. Doubting His presence can sometimes be due to the Enemy intensifying a trial that is tempting me to turn away from Father God. Other times, I believe Father God is preparing me; He's getting my character ready for more to come.

As our Father, God knows the character we need to fulfill His plans for us (Jeremiah 29:11). We need strength, developing grit for the storms ahead. A good father prepares his daughter for her future, teaching her skills she'll need for survival. He doesn't allow only ease to come her way, because she could lack the persistence and resilience needed to run her life race well (Philippians 3:14).

Father God has created good for us *and* He knows He's not the only one with a plan. Our enemy does too. Satan's agenda is to steal, kill, and destroy (John 10:10). Our Father doesn't want us ignorant of the two plans of the two kingdoms.

Read Psalm 66:12 again. Do you see that from the place of testing comes a new place of abundance? Of good?

In times of testing, it can feel like Father God is gone. David wrote, "Even though I walk through the darkest valley, I will fear no evil, for you are with me; your rod and your staff, they comfort me" (Psalm 23:4). Our Father isn't gone! In fact, He is nearer than He has ever been.

Experiencing Father God's Presence

Have you experienced the trauma of being abandoned or betrayed? When life hurts, we may question the Father's faithfulness. Perhaps you've questioned: *Are You just like my earthly parent? Just when I need You most, are You leaving me?* As we process how others have failed us, we can learn to trust that Father God never will. He can't fail. He is our fail-proof Father (Deuteronomy 31:6).

Growing Stronger

Read all of Psalm 66. Like the psalmist says in verse 16, declare by writing below what God has done for you.

2

God Is with You and Delights in You

MICHELLE

*The LORD your God is with you, the Mighty
Warrior who saves. He will take great delight in
you; in his love he will no longer rebuke you, but
will rejoice over you with singing.*

ZEPHANIAH 3:17

I just feel so special. I wish moments like these could last forever, I
thought the night my now husband told me he loved me for the very
first time. I saw the delight in his eyes and felt the love in his heart.
Moments where we feel loved fuel our hearts and remind us of the love
Father God has for us.

Have you had a moment where you felt God's love so completely
that it created a peaceful feeling throughout your body, mind, and soul?
Or maybe our heavenly Father's love moved you to tears because you
were so overwhelmed that the creator of the universe sees you and loves
you, and there is nothing you will ever have to do to earn His love.

This type of unconditional love is what the Father heart of God is
all about. As I look back over my life, I remember times when I felt this
love. Once after hearing a message about God's love, we sang "Jesus
Loves Me" and it was different from all the other times I'd sung it before
because I realized that God's love wasn't a broad, "for all of us" love but
personal for me, Michelle. Another time, I was at a church camp during
a time of silence. I sat lakeside, looking at a lit cross on the other side.

In my spirit, I felt God's love; I smile upon that memory. While a spiritual setting can help, focusing our mind's attention solely on Him and then opening ourselves to His affection are the keys to experiencing God's presence. Our divine Father can stream His presence, and we can connect with His Holy Spirit anytime and anywhere because He is in us.

Experiencing Father God's Presence

Spend some time reminding yourself of your own "God moments" where you experienced His love and presence. If you haven't felt the intense presence of God, you might consider attending a revival or church retreat/camp. Or, if you are in a quiet place, ask Him to reveal Himself to you right now.

Growing Stronger

Find a quiet place where you can be alone and set a timer on your phone for two minutes. Father God is omnipresent, so take a moment to acknowledge His presence with you. Breathe in deeply while counting to four, hold your breath for four counts, and then let all the air out of your body. As you take deep breaths, seek the face of God, reminding yourself who He is. You might begin with words like *Lover of my Soul*, *Light of the World*, *Savior*, *Almighty*, *Grace Giver*, *my Defender*, or *my Shelter*.

3

Encircled

LYNN

You have encircled me; you have placed your hand on me.

PSALM 139:5 CSB

I just needed to be held.

I didn't want to talk. I didn't want to hear "it's going to be okay." I wasn't ready for that. I just wanted to be held. So as my body shook and tears fell, my friend simply held me.

In the Psalms, I can usually find a passage describing exactly what I feel or what I really need to hear and know. Psalm 139 is one of those that helps in times when I'm feeling uncertain and even doubting that Father God really cares for me. The psalmist says, "You hem me in" in the New International Version. In the Christian Standard Bible, it says, "You have encircled me."

When I read "encircle," my thoughts immediately go to being wrapped in arms—our Father God's arms. In fact, in verse 4 the psalmist says, "Before a word is on my tongue you, LORD, know it completely." *Before.* With Father God, I really don't have to talk because He already knows and He is already there, right in the middle of my sorrow, my pain, and my joy, experiencing every moment of every second with me. Before I ask Him to comfort me, before I even know that I need comforting, Father God is there, encircling me.

One of the words translated as "presence" here in Psalm 139 is the

Hebrew word **mippaneka**. This word means "face."* The psalmist is trying to tell us that Father God is not only near or in the same room, He is as close as our face.

While arms wrapped around us are what we want, sometimes a friend or family member isn't able to be near to hold us. Father God is always available. As we grow in our trust of Him, we mature and we turn to Him, not as our last chance for comfort but as our first choice.

Experiencing Father God's Presence

Close your eyes and envision the arms of Father God encircling you.

Growing Stronger

Read all of Psalm 139 out loud. Which verse do you need to meditate on today? Text this to yourself or put it in a place you'll see it often. Glance at it throughout the day and if possible, say it out loud with your name in it, reminding yourself Father God is face-to-face with you today.

---

* *Strong's Concordance*, lexicon 6440: *face, faces*

4

God Goes Before You

MICHELLE

Do not be afraid or discouraged, for the LORD
will personally go ahead of you. He will be with
you; he will neither fail you nor abandon you.

DEUTERONOMY 31:8 NLT

As I've mentioned, I am the oldest of four kids in my family. Two of my closest friends in elementary school both had older sisters. I wished I had one too. Since I didn't have an older sibling, there were traditions in our middle and high school that I didn't know about. One was that parents sent flowers to wish their girls luck when they tried out for cheer and pep squad. But because I was the first in my family on the squad and my mom hadn't grown up in this community, we didn't know it was something we should do. I remember being the only girl who wasn't holding a flower, making tryouts an even more nerve-racking experience. This was just one of the many times I wished I'd had someone to do my hair and makeup and talk to me about how to navigate high school.

Like a big sister, God can go before us, preparing a way for kingdom tasks He calls us to. Often, I wondered why I participated in certain activities when I was young, but I later discovered these very activities prepared me to be a Christian speaker and writer. I also experienced God going before me by connecting me with people who had been where I was headed. I gained confidence in facing the unknown through their gifts of time, wisdom, and encouragement.

Experiencing Father God's Presence

Father, thank You for walking beside me and going before me in all that I do. I know I can take the next right step no matter how intimidated I might be because You have already prepared a way for me. Help me to move forward confidently, trusting in You to guide my steps and direct me along the crossroads of life.

Growing Stronger

Decisions are hard to make, but not deciding rarely helps us grow. When you come to the next life crossroad, force yourself to move a step in any direction, trusting that if you make what seems to be the wrong choice, God will not waste it. Trust your heavenly Father to use even the closed doors you face for your good.

5

Even There

LYNN

*Where can I go from your Spirit? Where can I flee
from your presence? If I go up to the heavens, you
are there; if I make my bed in the depths, you are
there. If I rise on the wings of the dawn, if I settle
on the far side of the sea, even there your hand
will guide me, your right hand will hold me fast.*

PSALM 139:7–10

ven there. Say those two words out loud. *Even there.*
I have had many occasions in my life when I've needed to know
Father God was with me there:

- When I sat in the hospital parking deck on my birthday,
  having left my father's bedside as he was dying. Even there, my
  heavenly Father was with me.
- When our daughter was taken to an emergency room after a
  life-threatening car accident and we were many miles away.
  Even as we sped down the highway, Father God was with us.
- When I sensed Father God giving me new plans for my life after
  high school, plans that were different than I had thought or
  imagined. He was there, even though it was scary.

I would imagine you have given the reply, "I'm hanging in there"
when someone asks, "How are you doing?" Yet in Psalm 139:7–10, who
is doing the action? Who is the one responsible for being there, guiding,
and holding? My friend Cheri Fletcher pointed this out in one of her

posts.* It's Father God. He is doing the holding. We're not hanging in there; we're being held in there.

Wherever I am, Father God will hold on to me. Wherever I am going, He is there already, so I do not have to fear.

Experiencing Father God's Presence

Is there a place—a physical place or even an emotional space—where it is hard to picture the Father being there with you? There are some spaces where it can be hard picturing God being *even there*, but He *is*:

- When I wonder if anyone cares, even there, You are with me.
- When I was assaulted, even there, You were with me.
- When I sinned or stumbled, even there, You never left me.

Now, not because you feel it but because God's Word says it's true, fill in this blank with that place for you. Then speak these words to yourself: "Even there, _____, You are with me."

Growing Stronger

Do you have a memory of when you knew that Father God was with you? Write out this memory in the space below or in your journal. Use it as a reminder to your future self that your Father is always with you.

_____

_____

_____

_____

_____

---

* You can find this post at https://cherifletcher.com/being-held
-in-there-when-jesus-chooses-to-touch-grab-hold-us/.

6

God's Presence in a Still, Small Voice

MICHELLE

> The LORD said, "Go out and stand on the
> mountain in the presence of the LORD, for the
> LORD is about to pass by." Then a great and
> powerful wind tore the mountains apart and
> shattered the rocks before the LORD, but the
> LORD was not in the wind. After the wind there
> was an earthquake, but the LORD was not in the
> earthquake. After the earthquake came a fire,
> but the LORD was not in the fire. And after the
> fire came a gentle whisper.

1 KINGS 19:11-12

After discovering all the other prophets had been killed, Elijah—a prophet in the Old Testament—felt alone and abandoned, and feared for his life. The stress of all the trauma caused his body to collapse. Can you imagine knowing you were doing the will of God and experiencing results like these? Would you be tempted to give up? I know I would. I can be pretty dramatic with God. I'd probably beg for an out, a way to escape, and cry out in confusion and desperation. We long for God to display His power and might in moments like these. We hope for signs and wonders like Daniel being delivered in the lion's den (Daniel 6:22). Mighty winds, earthquakes, and fires appeal to us as grand gestures fit for a mighty God.

Like Elijah, we need time to rest, physical and spiritual nourishment, and time alone so that we don't miss God even in His micromovements. As we quietly retreat, wait, and listen, we can trust God will speak.

Experiencing Father God's Presence

Father, as we live day to day on this earth, it's easy to feel alone and desperate for deliverance. Help us to resist the temptation to live distracted lives that drown out Your voice. Give us ears to listen so that we don't miss Your whispers. Amen.

Growing Stronger

Ask other Christians about times when God's direction was shouted clearly at them. Have them tell you about other times when His voice was quiet but they still recognized it was Him. When I was a kid, my dad shared this story with me. While working for mission control at NASA in his twenties, he continuously struggled with the tension between science and faith. One night alone in his apartment, my dad asked Father God to reveal Himself to him and prove He was real. That night God answered my dad's cry and his life was forever changed.

1

My First Choice

LYNN

If I say, "Surely the darkness will hide me and the light become night around me," even the darkness will not be dark to you; the night will shine like the day, for darkness is as light to you.

PSALM 139:11–12

I was in middle school and I was afraid of the dark. I'm sure my friends had long outgrown this fear, but not me.

By day, my attic-style bedroom was the coolest. I loved everything about it . . . except one thing. The night.

At night, I was alone. At night, everything was hidden. At night, this place felt spooky and scary. In the dark, my mind made up stories—people hidden in the oversized cupboards and closet. The half walls that created individual spaces for me and my sisters' beds now hid sections of my room I couldn't see. From day to night, the room didn't change, but I did. The confidence I had slipped away with the sun.

In Psalm 139:11–12, David likens Father God's presence to lightness and darkness. No matter what is taking place with the time of day and the light, the presence of God never changes. What changes is what we can see.

David, who wrote Psalm 139, understood this well. "If I say . . ." David realizes his words about his situation have power in his mind. He knows God is with him no matter what. David follows with, "Even the darkness will not be dark to you." When all we can see and all we can feel is darkness, Father God's presence is still there. He hasn't gone anywhere. "The night will shine like the day, for darkness is as light to you."

Even in the darkest moments of life, He is with you. When you walk down your school's hall unnoticed, when your bank account and gas tank are empty, when your home is cold, when love seems to have slipped away, when anger and tension have stolen the laughter and joy and what brought you joy no longer does, even then, His light is with you. He dwells in us and moves through us.

We want to *feel* the joyful presence of Father God all the time, but even when we don't feel, see, touch, or hear Him, He is with us. He is with you. In the darkness or in the light, He is there.

Experiencing Father God's Presence

What would it look like for you to begin to train yourself to turn to Him first when you feel alone or scared?

Growing Stronger

Our faith cannot be based on our feelings. If it is, when we don't experience God, our faith will fail. Commit Psalm 139:11–12 to memory so that on the days when the feelings fail, you know in your heart that God is still with you and for you.

8

God's Presence Fills Us with Joy

MICHELLE

You make known to me the path of life; you will fill me with joy in your presence, with eternal pleasures at your right hand.

PSALM 16:11

Often in interviews people ask me the difference between **joy** and **happiness**. While we often use these words interchangeably, I define *happiness* as something you get a certain amount of when you are born and then the rest is impacted by your life choices and experiences. *Joy*, being a fruit of the Spirit, is more internal and can be created in our hearts, minds, and bodies by being in God's presence by ourselves or during group worship.

We can also experience joy by practicing mindfulness. When we are mindful of God's presence and bring all our senses into the present, joy can be felt because we momentarily let go of our past guilt, current grief, and future worries.

Experiencing Father God's Presence

If the practice of mindfulness is new to you, find a quiet place where you feel completely safe to begin learning it. It can, however, be practiced anywhere.

Take a few deep breaths and focus on God's presence. Remind yourself of who He is. Allow the air to fill you and try to breathe in deeply, hold your breath for a few moments, and then breathe out slowly until all the air exits your lungs. Continue breathing deeply and then describe in detail five things you see. Keep practicing deep breaths and while closing your eyes, notice four things you hear. Follow this with three things you can touch, two things you can smell, and one thing you can taste.

Now dwell on a moment in time when you were really happy and knew you were experiencing God's blessing. Use all of your senses to take yourself fully into that spirit-filled moment. Thank God that you can experience His joy anytime and anywhere.

Growing Stronger

Make a list of at least ten joyful life moments you've experienced. If you struggle with this assignment, you might go back and look at some photos. Sometimes when answers evade you, it can be that life has been really hard or you've recently experienced significant trauma. It can also happen when you are struggling with hopelessness and darkness or depression. If those feelings have lasted more than two weeks, please seek help from a licensed mental health professional.

And if you are struggling, remember that sometimes we need direction and encouragement to allow someone to help us cope and reclaim our hope. If you are really stuck, it will take time to recover. Over the years, I've learned to be more patient with myself, knowing that the joy will come again as my heart, mind, spirit, and body heal.

9

Still My Shaking Heart

LYNN

I lift up my eyes to the mountains—where does my help come from? My help comes from the LORD, the Maker of heaven and earth.

PSALM 121:1–2

Sitting in my church seat—head bent, eyes shut—tears dripped down my cheeks. Starting as a trickle, they quickly turned into a torrent. The shaking of my shoulders gave me away, evidence I was weeping. I was doing my best to be silent, to keep my pain a secret. Once I opened my eyes, I realized I wasn't alone. While I was focused on my fears, a friend had come close and placed her arm around me. The arm wrapped around my shoulder felt like a hug wrapped around my heart.

My friend Caris Snider describes anxiety as an elephant sitting on our chest. When anxiety is heavy, our hearts, our minds, and our guts tremble from the weight of overwhelm. Living in survival mode, we forget to look to the Lord for help.

Do you ever talk to yourself? I do. In today's Scripture passage, I picture the writer as worried and worn out, talking to himself: "I lift up my eyes to the mountains—where does my help come from?" (Psalm 121:1).

When we feel sure no one understands, the natural thing to do is continually analyze our thoughts and interactions. Yet here, the writer reminds himself: "My help comes from the LORD, the Maker of heaven and earth" (v. 2). Not only does the writer name his helper, he also reminds himself of the magnitude of who his helper is. His helper is a friend, like the friend who put their arm around me. Yet even better than a human friend, our helper is the all-powerful One. When we remind ourselves that we're not alone and that the presence of the Maker of heaven and earth is our help, His presence can calm our shaking hearts. His presence instills hope for our overwhelming trouble.

Experiencing Father God's Presence

Physical movement can sometimes help when troubles overwhelm us. Simply look up at the clouds and the sun. God's creation can be a wonderful reminder of Father God's powerful presence right in the middle of the hard. Looking up and out at everything God has made can reset our hearts and remind us of just how big our Father God is compared to our problem. If you have time, take a blanket outdoors in the day or the evening, lie down, and look up, searching for evidence that God is near. Raise your hands to the sky or fall to your knees to thank Him for His presence with you.

Growing Stronger

Read all eight verses of Psalm 121. Make two lists below—one of the things Father God will do and one of things Father God will not do.

10

God's Presence Gives Us Rest

MICHELLE

And He said, "My presence shall go with you, and I will give you rest."

EXODUS 33:14 NASB

In this verse God is talking to Moses, who is leading the Israelites out of slavery in Egypt. Egypt was dominated by Pharaoh and his men, who treated the Lord's people harshly. The slightest resistance often resulted in death. Do you think it was easy for Moses to sleep at night knowing God's mission for him? Father God was asking Moses to publicly confront Pharaoh and demand he let God's people go free from slavery. As someone who'd been adopted into Pharaoh's family and grown up around the palace, Moses probably knew that Pharaoh's army would make every effort to prevent the Israelites' escape. Talk about the unknown. He had no idea how they would ever get out. God not only promised that His presence would be with him moment by moment, but that Moses would receive rest in the midst of his mission.

Leaving my newly acquired teaching job to attend seminary and pursue my counseling degree wasn't dangerous, but I did feel like Moses in that I didn't see how God could make a way. Sitting in my Sunday school teacher's kitchen, I wept as she asked me if it wasn't the right time, or if I lacked the faith to believe God would provide. My missionary parents lived overseas then, leaving me feeling like I was without a safety net. In my heart I knew the time had come, so I stepped out in faith. Within a year, God led me to a job as a nanny, which paid my small amount of bills and gave me the flexibility to attend school and study. I received a teaching assistant position at a Bible college that included a tuition waiver. Next, one of my loans was forgiven due to previous years of teaching summer school. As I stepped out in faith, God made a way where there seemed to be no way (Isaiah 43:19). God not only provided the rest I needed by providing for my needs, but I also slept peacefully that entire season of my life.

Experiencing Father God's Presence

Father, help me escape from any area of my life that I am enslaved. Thank You that I'm no longer under a yoke of impossible laws to follow. I can break free from the pressure of life's never-ending demands because I don't have to constantly strive to earn anything from You! Remind me I am free in Christ (Galatians 5:1). In Your Son's precious name, amen.

Growing Stronger

Ask God to prepare you with rest for the times He will ask you to step out in faith and rely solely on His presence. If you'd like to learn more about your rest style, take Dr. Saundra Dalton-Smith's Personal Rest Assessment (https://www.restquiz.com), which is based on principles from her book *Sacred Rest*.

11

Never, Never, Never

LYNN

*"All those the Father gives me will come to me,
and whoever comes to me I will never drive away."*

JOHN 6:37

When you're afraid that you might say the wrong thing, sometimes the best thing to do is walk away. I did that a time or two when my kids were growing up. Furious over . . . Well, I can't remember what it was. I was scared I would say something I would regret. So, instead of giving *them* a time-out, I gave myself one.

While it seemed like the right decision, I wonder if my walking away felt like rejection.

I read John 6:37 today, where Jesus reassures His followers that there is nothing they can do to cause Him to walk away.

Nothing. Absolutely nothing.

You may have heard your whole life, "God is always with you," so you think, *Of course He is.* And yet, there can be a corner of our minds that wrestles with believing it's really true. *Nothing can cause Him to reject me?* Depression, guilt, ignoring Him for a season, and busyness can create roadblocks in our minds as we wrestle with our faith.

Knowing God will never leave us can be especially hard if we've grown up in an environment where acceptance seemed to be based on what we do. Let's try something together. Fill in this blank: What if I _____? Even if you filled in this blank with something you think is a sinful, repulsive action, John 6 tells you God's answer would still be the same.

I will never reject you, He says.

Even if I _____?

Even then, He says. *I will never reject you.*

In the Amplified version of the Bible, John 6:37 is translated as "All that My Father gives Me will come to Me; and the one who comes to Me I will most certainly not cast out [I will never, never reject anyone who follows Me]." That's a lot of nevers!

Father God is driving home His point. He will never reject us because Jesus is our way. His presence is always with those who come to Him.

Experiencing Father God's Presence

Maybe you have done something or have had thoughts that have pressured you to think, *How could God still be with me when I* _____?"

Say today's verse out loud to remind your heart and mind of what is true: "All that My Father gives Me will come to Me; and the one who comes to Me I will most certainly not cast out [I will never, never reject anyone who follows Me]" (AMP). If you are still experiencing thoughts that Father God cannot accept you because of a particular sin, take some time to focus on this promise Jesus makes to us: *I will never reject you.*

Growing Stronger

Look up Psalm 103:12, Isaiah 38:17, and Micah 7:19. In these verses, what does Father God have to say about our sin?

12

God's Presence Provides Comfort

MICHELLE

Even though I walk through the valley of the shadow of death, I will fear no evil, for you are with me; your rod and your staff, they comfort me.

PSALM 23:4 ESV

As a young adult, when I first sensed God calling me to England for a summer of mission work, it seemed impossible. The commissioning service I attended already had enough volunteers; there were no more funds available to support those volunteering to go. Also, the church we were to be helping felt that they had enough people for the task. Yet I persisted. In the spring, one of the three students who originally went returned, opening a place for me for a few weeks in the Forest of Dean, located in western England. In May, we heard from a youth evangelist who wanted my help with both his youth conferences and at a local church that housed his ministry offices.

While the obstacles for me to go began to clear, the ministry that was sending me started equipping me for the spiritual obstacles I would face. The Western England churches were surrounded by witches' covens that openly practice satanic worship. The churches would receive calls stating the witches were praying against our efforts. Encountering blatant evil was a challenge I felt ill-equipped to battle.

Father God, through various conversations, books, and teachings, revealed to me that we don't have to fear evil because He has promised to be with us. Repeatedly, I witnessed lives changed that summer. Much later in my life, when I returned to the church in England where we grew the youth group, nurtured a mom's group, ran the first kids' club that area experienced, and visited religion classes in surrounding schools, I wept when I saw the pews that held only a handful of us in leadership and few older women had been replaced with round tables filled with families and small children. The church had not only survived but was thriving. Unbelievably, I was recognized and asked to share my story. I told them about the two truths I'd learned emphatically that summer: "The one who is in you is greater than the one who is in the world" (1 John 4:4), and no weapon formed against us will stand (Isaiah 54:17).

Experiencing Father God's Presence

Take a moment to celebrate God's victories you've read in Scripture and throughout this devotional. If you have time, create a playlist of songs reminding you of God's powerful victories. One of my favorites that I learned before I left for England is "Victory Chant."*

Growing Stronger

Write on a sticky note "God is for me," "I am victorious in Christ," or something similar. Place it where you will see it often. If you have a chance, go outside and shout this truth as loud as you can. Yelling loudly can give you a dopamine hit and releases endorphins in the body.

---

* You can find this song on the album *The Lord Reigns* (Hosannah! Music: 1989). Lyrics by Joseph Vogels; worship leader Bob Fitts.

13

Over and Over and Over

LYNN

Who is a God like you, who pardons sin and forgives the transgression of the remnant of his inheritance? You do not stay angry forever but delight to show mercy. You will again have compassion on us; you will tread our sins underfoot and hurl all our iniquities into the depths of the sea. You will be faithful to Jacob, and show love to Abraham, as you pledged on oath to our ancestors in days long ago.

MICAH 7:18–20

Have you ever burnt your hand on a cooktop? We used to have a cooktop that was smooth and black but lit up with red circles when it was hot. When it began to cool off, the redness faded and the cooktop returned to black. Once, when wondering if the cooktop was warm, I touched it. (I know! Not a great idea!) Even though the top was no longer red, it was still warm. I'm pretty sure I burned some fingerprints off!

I've had relationships like that cooktop. Red-hot fights led to months of no communication. After some time passed, the arguments no longer burned in my memory. I reached back out only to be burned again.

We can think of God like that—retreating from us when we don't do what He wants or holding our sins against us. And yet, His Word tells us He is not like that at all. He is not like any human relationship.

Father God is quick to forgive and move past our sins and failures. "You do not stay angry forever," Micah 7:18 says. He does not hold a grudge; He doesn't stay mad or stay away.

Forgiving makes our Father happy. He delights in loving us . . . even when we've failed Him. Drawing us close is not a burden. It doesn't pain Him to be around us when we have done wrong. In fact, when we have done wrong and we ask for forgiveness, He has compassion on us! He throws our sins far from us so that we will not have anything separating us from Him. And the crazy thing is . . . He actually longs to communicate with us and doesn't punish us for the time when we were distant. When we purpose to love Him with all of our heart, His love and patience keep coming to us over and over and over.

Experiencing Father God's Presence

When we get in a fight with another person, a common reaction is to walk out of a room, hang up the phone, or stop texting. We cut off communication. Father God does just the opposite. He forgives and shows compassion. Below, write about how this love is different from what you have previously experienced.

_____

_____

_____

_____

_____

_____

Growing Stronger

Hosea 11 creates a beautiful but different picture of Father God's loving presence in our lives. What type of picture do you see in this chapter?

14

You Can Run, but You Can't Hide

MICHELLE

But Jonah rose to flee to Tarshish from the presence of the LORD. He went down to Joppa and found a ship going to Tarshish. So he paid the fare and went down into it, to go with them to Tarshish, away from the presence of the LORD.

JONAH 1:3 ESV

*H*as God ever asked you to do something and you wished you could just pass? Maybe you sensed Him asking you to give up something you wanted to keep. Maybe He asked you to speak to someone you don't know or serve where you felt very unequipped and unqualified. If you haven't felt something like that yet, give Him time. He will.

Jonah was asked to go to some very rebellious people with God's message to repent. He resisted. Jonah unsuccessfully tried to outrun God by ship and ended up in the belly of a giant fish until he relented.

The Lord creates growth and maturity in our lives by asking us to step out of our comfort zones. If we resist or delay, we lose out. Often our unfailing Father, who doesn't give up on us, creates similar opportunities, giving us a second chance to respond in obedience. Listening and obeying God has resulted in some of the most amazing experiences in my life, but they rarely come without fear and trembling (Philippians 2:12).

Experiencing Father God's Presence

Father, I don't want to land in a modern-day version of a fish's belly. I commit from this day forward to obey Your call even when it's scary and uncomfortable. Help me when I lack courage. In Jesus's name, amen.

Growing Stronger

Sometimes stepping out to obey God for a season seems easier than daily obedience. If someone has used the word *obey* in a harsh way, it might make you feel uncomfortable or even scared that you might get hurt. Using a Bible search engine, search the word **obey** and then look up those verses. What does obedience to your heavenly Father look and feel like based on the Scriptures you read?

_____

_____

_____

_____

_____

_____

_____

_____

_____

_____

_____

_____

15

He Is with Me

LYNN

A time to weep and a time to laugh, a time to mourn and a time to dance.

ECCLESIASTES 3:4

Have you ever noticed the various reactions and responses you encounter when you're hurting?

Recently, my family went through a season of suffering. During this heartbreaking time, I reached out to those who love me, to pray for me and help carry our heavy burden.

As I shared our story with friends, I received very different responses.

One friend immediately began to weep. Brokenhearted *for* us, she wept *with* me. She took me in her arms and held me. She eventually encouraged me to trust God and forgive, but her first move was to cry with me.

Another friend, while her heart was in a good place, skipped the grieving, heading straight to encouragement. Her words, while true, even scriptural, were untimely and landed painfully in my heart.

I sometimes wonder if as Jesus followers we think that if we don't immediately express faith for healing, belief for restoration, or hope for the future, we're demonstrating we don't have faith, belief, and hope. Or maybe we lean into the concept of "good vibes only," attempting to help the one grieving not get stuck in negativity.

Yet Scripture tells us in Ecclesiastes 3:1, "There is a time for everything, and a season for every activity under the heavens." One of these seasons and times is "a time to weep . . . a time to mourn" (v. 4).

Jesus demonstrates so beautifully with His presence how to enter into grieving and lamenting with those who are hurting. In John 11, His friend Lazarus has died. Jesus goes to His hurting friends: "When Jesus saw [Mary] weeping, and the Jews who had come along with her also weeping, he was deeply moved in spirit and troubled" (v. 33) Jesus allowed Mary's pain to impact Him. He was moved, even troubled. He wept (v. 35). His expression of emotion didn't indicate His lack of faith; He knew He would raise His friend from the dead. He had faith *and* He lamented. He wept, hurt, and felt for His friends.

The gift Jesus gave to His friends in the middle of their pain was His presence. He came and was with them.

When we're in pain, when we're grieving, we need people; we need support and empathy from family and friends. We also need to be aware that in the middle of our hurting, Father God is with us, wanting to comfort us.

Experiencing Father God's Presence

Ask Father God to help you to reach out to Him when your heart is hurting.

Growing Stronger

How can we receive comfort from the fact that Jesus is acquainted with grief (Hebrews 4:15)?

16

God's Presence in the Midst of Trauma

MICHELLE

Where can I go to escape your Spirit? Where can I flee from your presence?

PSALM 139:7 CSB

Believing that God is omnipresent challenges our physical eyes. Learning to see with spiritual eyes opens our senses to His presence at all times. When I'm working with trauma survivors, they often ask me if God's presence exists in the midst of a sexual assault. Current statistics from RAINN.org reveal that every nine minutes, a child experiences sexual abuse.[*] Second Samuel 13 reveals that David's own daughter Tamar was raped by her half brother. Her half brother died at the hands of her brother, who was determined to avenge her. The idea that God would be present and not intervene when one of His children is being violated distresses even the strongest believer.

This broken world is a far cry from heaven, where Father God's perfect will occurs. When I use a trauma intervention called EMDR (eye movement desensitization and reprocessing)[†] with women who've experienced pain at the hands of another, they sometimes choose God as their resource as we go through this therapy and experience something

---

[*] "Children and Teens: Statistics," RAINN, accessed March 26, 2024, https://www.rainn.org/statistics/children-and-teens.

[†] Find out more information about this therapeutic intervention at the EMDR International Association, https://www.emdria.org/.

called "bilateral stimulation." Bilateral stimulation is a physical process that helps the right brain (emotional side) connect with the left brain (logical side) in order to "unblock" negative memories so your mind can start reprocessing them and heal. It is often done by following a hand or ball with your eyes or feeling a pair of vibrating handles that you hold. A simple form of this is called "butterfly tapping," which is done by crossing your arms over your chest and tapping each shoulder with your hands, alternating at your chosen pace or rhythm. When we use this technique in the counseling office, it involves silent processing that for many of my Christian clients allows God to change the way their brain views an event and the beliefs they embraced about themselves during it.

Bringing God into the picture as we heal from past trauma releases His light into the darkest moments of our lives. Many clients report they hear His words of compassion toward them and anger at the one who did the harm to them. Our Father's presence doesn't make the bad good, but it can provide the healing we need to live no longer broken.

Experiencing Father God's Presence

Are there areas of darkness in your life that you believe God cannot enter? Invite Him in for just a moment. If the trauma or even a sin of your own seems too bad for God, seek help from a minister or Christian counselor to help you begin the healing process.

Growing Stronger

Read 2 Samuel 13:1–33. Ask God to protect women and children everywhere from sexual assault and trafficking. Learn about a sex trafficking ministry that you could pray for or support.

17

Never Going to Leave

LYNN

"Be strong and courageous. Do not be afraid or terrified because of them, for the LORD your God goes with you; he will never leave you nor forsake you."

DEUTERONOMY 31:6

I couldn't believe it was happening again. Another youth pastor, who I trusted and loved, was leaving our church. *Why do people I love keep leaving my life?*

Have you ever felt abandoned or left alone? I wonder if when you read Deuteronomy 31:6 there is a part of you that thinks, *Really, God? Will You really never leave me or forsake me? Because others have.* Neighbors move. Teachers get new jobs. Friends find other friends. Mentors move on. Coaches choose new opportunities. Grandparents die. Parents leave.

Except God. God, our true Father who created us, has never been in that list of those who have left you or deserted you, and He never will. Father God says, *I am different. I will not leave you. I will not desert you nor let you stand alone. In fact, it is impossible for Me to do so. I can't because leaving you vulnerable, unprotected, and without comfort, strength, or hope is completely against who I am. I am your constant companion.* He keeps this promise.

Experiencing Father God's Presence

Thank Father God for His promise to never leave or forsake you. Your prayer could sound something like this: Father, thank You that although relationships in my life are constantly changing, some coming and others going, You never leave. Open my eyes to see that every time someone left, You have remained there. Amen.

Growing Stronger

Deuteronomy 31:6 is not the only time God has promised to never leave us or forsake us. Read Genesis 28:15, Deuteronomy 4:31, Joshua 1:5, 1 Chronicles 28:20, and Hebrews 13:5 for additional reassurance of God's promise.

18

Thankful for God's Presence

MICHELLE

Let us come into his presence with thanksgiving;
let us make a joyful noise to him with songs of
praise!

PSALM 95:2 ESV

What is it about God's presence being in your life that fills your heart with joy? Maybe it's that you will never be lonely, which is something my grandmother—who lived to be ninety-seven—shared with me. Or as someone who talks out loud to themselves, I love having God to talk to even when no one is around. Knowing I have the attention of the creator of universe overrides my feelings of insignificance and reminds me I am special to Him. When I'm in a hurry, I often pray that He will help me locate jewelry, shoes, and other items I can't find. I also thank the Lord when those prayers are answered. Experiencing God doesn't have to be complicated and doesn't require stillness. Deuteronomy 4:29 promises that when we seek Him, we will find Him. When we delight in the heavenly Father's presence with thanksgiving, our brains spend less time focused on our worries.

If you live with others, you might create a gratitude jar with a few slips of paper and pen in a basket nearby. All of you can take time writing out your thoughts of gratitude that can be shared at mealtimes. These types of activities don't have to be reserved just for the Thanksgiving table. A group of teens in our area started a gratitude-to-God text chain where they share and celebrate His goodness together. I have asked clients in our offices to complete a Happiness Rating Scale* and then go home and practice daily gratitude for the next two weeks. When they return, I have them complete the quiz again. Almost always, their scores go up. They often remark that while they lacked awareness of the impact of their gratitude practice, completing this activity reinforced their desire to continue practicing gratitude on a regular basis.

Experiencing Father God's Presence

Start your next dedicated time with the Lord by specifically thanking Him for the ways He has shown up in your life in the last twenty-four hours.

Growing Stronger

Plan to get to church fifteen minutes early on a Sunday morning. Sit in your car or in the worship center before the service starts. In your mind, on paper, or on a phone or tablet, make a list of things you are thankful for directed to God. If you need help, start with your physical needs, then move to the people who bless your life and how they do so, and continue including unseen things.

---

* The "Happiness Rating Scale Quiz" can be found at https://www.happy -relationships.com/ (copyright 2009 by Richard E. Hamon II).

19

You Forgive

LYNN

When we were overwhelmed by sins, you forgave our transgressions.

PSALM 65:3

D o you ever have conversations with your parents about their lives when they were growing up? My mom shared with me that my grandfather was a man who would sometimes give gifts to his children, but when my mom did something wrong and he became angry, he would take away his gift.

When my mom came to know Father God, she was afraid her heavenly Father would do the same—take away the gift of salvation when she sinned. She lived trying to never do anything wrong. As she grew in her faith, her fear waned as she learned Jesus's death took away her sins in the past, the present, and the future. He would never take away her salvation or His forgiveness.

Our good Father doesn't want us to sin because He doesn't want us to hurt. He doesn't want our relationship with Him damaged as a result of suffering the natural consequences of earthly pain when we make poor choices. But we don't have to fear our Father when we sin and make mistakes. He knows what we are made of; He's the One who made us! He knows we're human and incapable of being perfect.

Maybe you haven't experienced this type of grace—a kindness and favor that isn't won or given when you've earned it. In fact, maybe the pattern you're used to is the opposite. When you've messed up, you've been reminded over and over, "You never could do anything right."

"You're irresponsible." "You've always been that way." When your record of shortcomings is recited, you can wonder if maybe you won't ever change or you can't. And just that easily . . . your eyes are off your Father, who forgives, restores, and makes all things new, including you and me.

When we ask for forgiveness, our Father moves on. The other people in your life may not, but Father God is not like that! He forgives when we confess our sins and accept His forgiveness, which was provided through the death of Jesus.

Experiencing Father God's Presence

Father, while others see my actions and assume what is in my heart, You see my heart and understand my actions. Align them both with You, O Lord—my heart and my actions. Amen.

Growing Stronger

Say Psalm 65:3 out loud three times: "When we were overwhelmed by sins, you forgave our transgressions."

20

Are You Thirsty for His Presence?

MICHELLE

O God, You are my God; I shall seek You earnestly;
my soul thirsts for You, my flesh yearns for You,
in a dry and weary land where there is no water.

PSALM 63:1 NASB

*I*f you spend any time watching the news these days, it's easy to become anxious. I had a client who lowered her anxiety scale score in half by reducing how much time she spent looking at screens. I asked her, "What if instead of ruminating or obsessing over the problems in our world, you spent at least the same amount of time focused on the bigness of God?" As she worked at balancing her God focus with her worries about our world, she reported back that she wanted God to fill more of her mental energy. She became thirsty for more time focused on her divine Father.

Jerry Jenkins, who wrote the famous evangelist Billy Graham's biography, once shared in a speech that he'd asked Billy why he had open Bibles all over his home. Billy replied that just like snacking on food throughout the day, he wanted to have open reminders to snack on the Word of God. When I lived in the dorms at Baylor University, we placed transparent page holders in all the bathroom stalls. We took turns writing and printing out devotions or Scriptures to slide in the holders so we could be encouraged throughout our day. I keep devotionals like the one you are reading in our home bathrooms for the same reason.

In the counseling office, clients battle worries racing through their heads that feel overwhelming. When we write our negative thoughts out on a piece of paper, draw out future fears with art, or play out past hurts in a sand tray, we become bigger and whatever was running through our head seems smaller. Recognizing that Father God is with us during these exercises shrinks our negativity exponentially. The more we focus on God our Father, the more we want to make Him part of our lives, because all things grow dim in the presence of our heavenly Father!

Experiencing Father God's Presence

Stop and set a timer for one minute and practice being in God's presence. As you postpone what you were going to do, acknowledge that God is with you in this moment even though you can't physically see Him. Take a deep breath and try tuning into His peace and love for you. You can do this by focusing your mind on Him and reminding yourself of truths that you've learned in these devotions. Ask Him to help you increase your time focused on Him in the next 1,439 minutes you now have left in a twenty-four-hour period of time.

Growing Stronger

Set three daily alarms on your phone and label them *Father*. When they go off, set a timer for one minute and practice envisioning your heavenly Father smiling down on you with loving eyes, ever ready to help.

For the One Ready to Walk with Jesus

MICHELLE

Surrender your entire life to Him. Surrender is a decision that you can take deeper with time. You might start by giving Him the agenda for your life. As you wake up, you might ask Him to lead you through your day. When you get a paycheck or think about buying something, you can thank Him for providing for you and ask for help with spending your money wisely. If you are struggling with a relationship, you might ask Him to give you wisdom to navigate it or the strength to let it go if it's not good for you or isn't pleasing to Him.

Matthew 16:24 talks about denying yourself and following Jesus. Being a Christ follower involves choosing God's ways based on His Word over what may seem or feel right to you. If you've made the decision to surrender your life to Father God and haven't been baptized or don't remember your baptism, you might choose this external expression of your internal decision. Seek out being baptized at your local church.

Connect with Him daily. Use devotionals like this one; pick a book of the Bible like Proverbs, Psalms, one of the Gospels, Romans, Galatians, or Ephesians (use an audio version if you prefer); read through the New Testament in a year; listen to a daily Bible podcast; and in time, read through the Bible in a year. Memorize Scripture with a friend. Spend time being still, listening to worship music, and communicating with your Father through prayer. No matter what you do, as 1 Thessalonians 5:16 tells us, rejoice always.

Share His love with others. Join a prayer group, use a prayer app, share prayer requests with friends, send someone who needs encouragement a Bible verse or audio prayer. Matthew 28:19 encourages us to share God's good news with others—and when we make that a natural part of our life, doing so becomes much easier.

Find a community to connect with. In-person praise and worship with others allows you to experience God's presence and empowers you to follow Christ throughout your week. Listening to someone who makes the Bible come alive with practical life application propels you toward days filled with encouragement, conviction, and inspiration. When we surround ourselves with a community, we can experience the wisdom of others talked about in Colossians 3:16.

Plug into a small group where you can be known. Hebrews 10:24–25 calls us to "spur one another on toward love and good deeds" by intentionally meeting with other Christ followers. Find a Bible study, attend a youth group, join or lead a college and career group, connect with your high school or college ministry on campus, ask someone you admire to lead a study and invite some friends, or if all else fails, start your own peer-led group.

Select a place to serve. Service not only improves your mental health, it allows you to connect with older adults in the church and have one-on-one time and conversations. Whether you like working with kids, enjoy greeting people, love sharing the gospel message and inviting others to follow Christ, are willing to be part of a prayer team, would enjoy driving an elderly person to church, or feel most comfortable helping behind the scenes, congregations need your gifts.

Taking a spiritual gifts inventory can help. Team Ministry has a free one available (https://gifts.churchgrowth.org/spiritual-gifts-survey). As you mature, you may want to move into a leadership position to further develop these gifts. And remember: as Romans 12:4–8 makes clear, we all have different gifts by design. How you are meant to serve will likely look different than what others around you are called to do—but when all of us use the gifts He's given us, lives are changed.

Topical Index

About the Authors

*P*rofessional counselor for twenty-five years, **Michelle Nietert** is the clinical director of Community Counseling Associates and is the bestselling coauthor of *Managing Your Emojis*, the Bringing Big Emotions to a Bigger God series (including *God, I Feel Sad* and *God, I Feel Scared*), *Loved & Cherished*, and the award-winning book for adults *Make Up Your Mind*. A popular speaker on topics regarding mental health, faith, and parenting, Michelle is a frequent guest on national television and radio and hosts the *Raising Mentally Healthy Kids* podcast. Michelle and her husband, Drew, have been married over twenty years and have two teenagers. Connect with Michelle at YourMentalHealthCoach.com to discover resources or learn more about her counselor network. She also loves interacting on Instagram (@michellenietert) or Facebook (@MichelleNietert).

*T*he message you'll find woven throughout **Lynn Cowell**'s teaching and writing is how to find confidence in Christ. Her latest Bible study for women is *Esther: Seeing Our Invisible God in an Uncertain World*, and for kids, *Managing Your Emojis: 100 Devotions for Kids*. She also writes for Proverbs 31 Ministries' Encouragement for Today. Lynn calls North Carolina home, where she and her husband, Greg, and the occasional backyard deer are adjusting to life as "just us." Along with their three adult children and their spouses, the Cowells love hiking, making homemade pizza, and anything combining chocolate and peanut butter.

Loved and Cherished

Sometimes we think what we do, what we say, or what others say about us changes our worth. We worry that we must be perfect to be loved. But as children of God, we can be confident that we are loved, cherished, and secure because God loves us no matter what. This devotional written for girls 8 to 12 includes Bible verses about God's love, thoughts

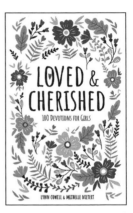

about those verses, questions for journaling or thinking, and ideas for ways to talk with God just as you are. When you live as God's chosen girl, you can hold your head high.

Managing Your Emojis

If you're feeling big feelings, you are not alone. God created you to feel emotions. But occasionally our emotions get intense, and it seems like they are running us. God wants to come alongside you when you feel sad, scared, mad, or unhappy. He promises to be there for you! This 100-day devotional helps you face your feelings, recognize it's OK to feel

the way you do, and know the empowerment of God's Word and His unconditional love and understanding.

Available wherever books are sold!